NORMAN SPENCER

WHAT
PRICE
SUCCESS

ONE MAN'S 34-YEAR
SEARCH FOR HIS GI FATHER

NORMAN SPENCER

WHAT
PRICE
SUCCESS

ONE MAN'S 34-YEAR
SEARCH FOR HIS GI FATHER

MEREO
Cirencester

Mereo Books

1A The Wool Market Dyer Street Cirencester Gloucestershire GL7 2PR
An imprint of Memoirs Publishing www.mereobooks.com

What Price Success: 978-1-86151-343-4

First published in Great Britain in 2014
by Mereo Books, an imprint of Memoirs Publishing

The address for Memoirs Publishing Group Limited can be found at
www.memoirspublishing.com

The Memoirs Publishing Group Ltd Reg. No. 7834348

The Memoirs Publishing Group supports both The Forest Stewardship Council® (FSC®) and
the PEFC® leading international forest-certification organisations. Our books carrying both the
FSC label and the PEFC® and are printed on FSC®-certified paper. FSC® is the only
forest-certification scheme supported by the leading environmental organisations including
Greenpeace. Our paper procurement policy can be found at
www.memoirspublishing.com/environment

Typeset in 11/15pt Bembo
by Wiltshire Associates Publisher Services Ltd. Printed and bound in Great Britain by
Printondemand-Worldwide, Peterborough PE2 6XD

Dedicated to my mother, Doris Spencer,
who loved children.

CONTENTS

ACKNOWLEDGEMENTS

My special thanks to Norma Jean Clarke-McCloud for her unselfish dedication to helping others; to LeAnn Fields, a brilliant researcher and friend of humanity; Shirley McGlade, whose legal campaign eventually overcame the US military Privacy Act; and the late Pamela Winfield MBE, whose good works have inspired so many GI children to seek and find their biological fathers.

Contributors:
David Jackson
Tony Watson
Lynn M. Gregory
Donald P. Bolce
Peter Gripton

and others too numerous to mention, but not too few to have my appreciation and heartfelt thanks.

CHAPTER ONE

THE GIRL FROM THE NORTH COUNTRY

My story begins in the early years of the 20th century, in the market town of Barnard Castle in the north–eastern English county of Durham.

The town has long been known locally as "Barney". The main entrance to the town, Galgate, a wide boulevard combined with an equally spacious High Street, forms a unique tapestry in this town of 5,000 inhabitants. This is a close-knit community which has evolved around the 12th century Norman castle.

The River Tees rushes by beneath these ancient ruins, forming a natural border between the counties of Durham and Yorkshire. In the background beyond are the rolling green fields neatly bordered by centuries old dry stone walling.

In the midst of this peaceful setting my mother was born on April 26th 1909, to be christened Doris. She was the first child of John George and Susan Victoria Spencer, who lived in Coronation Street. My grandfather was usually referred to as George. He was a bicycle mechanic and had a partnership in a small cycle shop situated in Barnard Castle town centre.

Just over two years later, in July 1911, tragedy befell the Spencer family. Susan Spencer, while working in the garden, cut her finger and as a result, she contracted tetanus. This affliction resulted in her premature death and sent her husband George spiralling into bouts of anxiety and depression. This had a cumulative negative effect upon his business partnership and family life. As a result of this, his ability to care for his young daughter was severely impaired and a decision had to be made regarding her future care. Doris was sent to live with her paternal grandparents.

Gradually George Spencer recovered from his trauma, although his finances had been severely damaged by this experience. His recovery was aided by meeting Ethel Holmes. A pleasant, dynamic, middle–class lady, she proved to be the ideal person to help him restore normality in his life.

In April 1916 George and Ethel were married and began a new life together. Now Doris was able to return to the household from her grandparents' home and be raised by her new stepmother.

In June 1921 a baby boy, to be christened Peter, was born. My mother now had a half-brother and was growing up in a stable, secure family.

In "Barney" around that time, things had gradually returned to normal following World War 1. Normality at that time was, in effect, a return to the status quo, and my mother was in the midst of this. I believe she would have left school at the age of 15 (or possibly 14) and taken employment in or around her home town at that time. However she developed a yearning to break out of this sedate but secure lifestyle, and she developed a skill which would enable her to do this. Having a great affinity with children, she saw future employment opportunities working as a nanny; it would also be a means to see and experience other parts of the country. Eventually she left the family home at the age of 19, having secured a post in the seaside resort of Scarborough, some 45 miles away.

As a live-in nanny she would have shared in the life of her employer's family more than maids and kitchen staff, and enjoyed a higher status. Such posts are, by their very nature, transient. Once the children grow up, the need for a nanny is removed.

This experience served my mother well and at the age of 21, she realised a long-held ambition to see more of the world by securing a post "down south" in the English capital, London. My mother was a fun-loving person and this move, a big venture for a young woman in those times, must have been very exciting and character-forming.

In London she came to meet another young woman from the North East, Lesley Schubeler. Lesley's genealogy dated back to Norway. She had arrived in London in 1929 to seek the employment which would enable her to lead a better quality of life compared to the relative impoverishment of her home town, Newcastle.

The two young women quickly established a friendship which would endure for a lifetime. This duo - the "new kids in town" - shared a flat at No. 10 William Street in the Knightsbridge district of the city. A very wealthy area, it was a place where there was no lack of upper-class families seeking experienced nannies. The world renowned Massey's Domestic Agency in Baker Street was a conduit for such employment and my mother would use their services both then and in the years ahead.

At this time the country was still emerging from the worst

effects of the Great Depression. London, however, remained relatively affluent, and there was a great demand for new domestic staff. There is no doubt that life in the "big city" at that time would have been light years away from the scene in homely Barnard Castle.

As the decade drew on, Lesley Schubeler came to meet the love of her life, Arthur Watson. In 1936, as a result of her romance with Arthur, she left the shared flat to start married life in south-east London. Very soon after this situation-changing event, the flat was vacated, as my mother then took up employment as a live-in nanny to the two children of Mr and Mrs Peter Green of Kensington. For a time this new domestic situation was successful for all concerned, but the day eventually came when the Greens announced that their children had reached the age when a nanny was no longer required.

Although this did not come as a great surprise, it was still unwelcome news, as my mother had enjoyed her time in the Green household. In turn they were reluctant to lose her good services and offered her the chance to stay on as their cook.

Years later I was to learn, through my step-grandmother, how my mother had reacted to this offer. The reply to the Greens' request for her to cook for them was: "But madam, I don't know how to cook professionally - it's something I have never done".

The immediate reply was that they would send her, all expenses paid, to the world-famous Cordon Bleu College in London's West End. There she would be trained to carry out the culinary requirements of her prospective employers to the highest possible standard.

The Greens were great entertainers, putting on many dinner parties and other social events. Among the many guests were politicians like Rab Butler, entertainers like Richard Wattis and members of the nobility. Out in the kitchen my mother's newly-acquired skills were put to the test, and, from what she told me, she must have passed with flying colours. "Northern girl" Doris Spencer had made it in the big city, and the future was bright and exciting.

Then on September 1st 1939 Germany invaded Poland and the seeds of the Second World War began to germinate. Two days later Britain declared war on Germany, and some months later, my mother received official Government orders to leave her domestic post and commence work in a munitions factory just outside the confines of the metropolis.

Having to leave the Green household was a bitter blow, but it was no less serious than the situation now faced by thousands of other people as the influences of wartime began to take effect. My mother now had to find somewhere else to live, and eventually she secured accommodation in the Notting Hill district of the city.

Her hours at the factory filling explosives into the cartridges of tracer bullets were long and arduous, and there was always the risk of explosion from the materials involved. The safety and status of her previous employment were far removed from this new and unwanted situation. Now the country was at war, and away from the vast military operations every civilian contribution was vital if victory was eventually to be achieved.

During this time my mother travelled between the factory and her new residence. In her limited leisure time she would venture out to a public house, cinema or theatre.

At this time every journey, even the shortest one, was fraught with danger and my mother often related to me why this was so. The German Reich had decided to retaliate against the bombing raids on their cities, and they did so with a new form of terror. In addition to the conventional bombs being dropped by the Luftwaffe, a new invention, the unmanned V1 and V2 rockets, were being aimed at London from launch pads on the European mainland. These rockets would strike completely at random and explode upon the city's residents. It made no difference whether you were rich or poor, old or young, academic or illiterate - death from the skies was an ever-present danger. My mother often told me of the many instances when these attacks began and how she had to look for the safety of the nearest underground station and run down the steps.

In 1938 Peter Spencer, my mother's half-brother, had enrolled in the British Army. By the time hostilities had broken out the following year he was already a fully-trained professional soldier. Prior to D-Day in 1944, he made his way to London. I am not sure whether it was on leave or operations, but it seems he did meet up with my mother and they were able to socialise in some of the West London public houses. Once there they would have be able to catch up with the news of events and occasions happening back up north in "Barney".

After the initial invasion of Europe by the Allied Forces, Peter had travelled over with his army unit to the mainland. They then began to engage in the long trail of combat which was necessary in order to ensure eventual victory.

On the 11th of October 1944, from her Notting Hill flat, my mother sent an official army field post letter addressed to

Pvt. Peter Spencer. It read thus:

8, Northumberland Place
W2
11-10-44

Dear Peter,
Glad to receive your letter form also your field card. I haven't much news
we have not been sent to another factory yet but will be very soon. I
have had a couple of days off but could do with two months. I was in
the Windsor Clive the other day and the Bunch of Grapes the other
night. Hope Albert is still o. k. Also yourself. I am getting my photo
taken for Christmas so don't give up hope, well Pete cheerio for now,

Love from Doris.

I only know that she sent him this letter because I have it in my
possession. It was returned to her unopened. In ink somebody
had written diagonally across the envelope "Deceased" and this
had been confirmed by the standard official stamp which read:

IT IS REGRETTED THAT THIS ITEM COULD
NOT BE DELIVERED BECAUSE THE ADDRESSEE IS
REPORTED DECEASED

For my mother, like so many other people at that time, the war
had now become very personal, very real, and very cruel.

CHAPTER TWO

A CHILDHOOD ON THE MOVE

On October 14th 1944, Lincolnshire regiment Private Peter Spencer was killed by a land mine while carrying out an advanced night patrol near the Belgian/German border. He was just 23 years old. The only consolation my mother and her family up north would have had was the reported fact that death would have been instantaneous.

There is scant time for grieving during a time of war, and my mother just had to move on with her life and continue her work at the munitions factory. With the knowledge that her half-brother had become yet another statistic of the war, Christmas 1944 would be a hollow experience, eased only by having the courage to go out and make some social contact with the world outside her flat.

The springtime of 1945 eventually arrived and, although the war was continuing to be conducted, there was no doubt that the tide was turning in favour of the Allied forces. Final victory would just be a matter of time. With this upturn in prospect, my mother's work in the munitions factory was brought to an end, and she was redirected to work on the London Underground system as a porteress. She began at Baker Street, where, among her duties, was a requirement to operate the PA system and utter the classic words: "Mind the doors please". This would be broadcast before the departure of every train.

Eventually an order for my mother's transfer to Westbourne Park station was sent through. This new working venue was infinitely more convenient for her, as it was less than a mile from the Northumberland Place flat.

On May 7th 1945 the German military signed the document of unconditional surrender, and Europe was once more free. Although the war in the Pacific had yet to be concluded, the feeling prevailed that the worst was over and better times lay ahead.

The following day, May 8th, was declared "Victory in Europe Day" -VE Day. All democratic nations celebrated and the English capital, London, was no exception. This historic day brought the city to a standstill and it is certain that my mother would have joined in the celebrations, though I do not know exactly where.

That momentous day of joy was truly something to behold. Strangers embraced like long-lost brothers and sisters, grown men cried openly and the dark shadow of oppression was banished to the past, hopefully for all time. But amid all this euphoria there was something else on my mother's mind, and it was not going to go away, not on VE Day or the next day, not ever. She was already 19 weeks pregnant, and the man responsible had departed from her life, never to return.

On the 24th September at Paddington General Hospital, Doris Spencer, porteress, gave birth to a son, later to be christened Norman Peter. My arrival in the world was unheralded and unremarkable, apart from the fact that it happened at the time when a brave new post-war world was also being born.

Following my arrival we were transferred to a nearby hostel for single mothers which provided a vital refuge for young women without any ready means of family support. St Helena's Convalescent Home in Thorverton Road, NW1, was founded in Victorian times. In the adjacent chapel I was baptised by the local vicar, a thoughtful additional service supplementing the food and accommodation already provided by St Helena's.

The dedicated staff were angels in disguise. The stigma of being a single mother in that era produced pressures which today would be unimaginable.

For a brief time during the war years, my mother had lost contact with Lesley Watson. Following my birth, she contacted Lesley to tell her that she was now a single mother. Naturally my mother was very ill at ease with her new station in life and did not want most people to know she was an unmarried mother.

The ever-thoughtful Lesley then provided her with a small gift in the form of a modestly-priced wedding ring. In future, wherever she went, my mother would wear this ring, a matrimonial symbol used to deflect any future awkward and inquisitive questions.

However difficult her circumstances undoubtedly were, she seems never to have entertained the thought of having me adopted.

Overnight Miss Doris Spencer became War Widow Mrs Doris Spencer. This transformation did not however provide any additional income, pitiful as it would have been, in the shape of a war widow's allowance.

The fast-paced society of today may still harbour many faults, but thankfully, prejudice against the working, single unmarried mother is not one of them. It was not so in 1945. My mother had to choose the best option available to sustain us, and once again she entered domestic service, as a live-in cook. For a time late in 1945 she cooked for the Hoare family at their home in Lennox Gardens, Knightsbridge. The following year she took up a similar appointment with the Prideaux family (who will be mentioned again in a later chapter), whose residence, Hamsell Lake House, was near Eridge on the Kent/Sussex border.

The house stood in an elevated rural location with a large garden, an orchard and a lake, surrounded by trees right up to the water's edge. One of my earliest recollections was of walking around the edge of the lake in summer, listening to the roar of the water as it cascaded through the sluice gates.

The Prideaux family were founders of the Goldsmiths' Company, an organisation which is one of the twelve great livery companies of the City of London. The lady of the house, Marion Prideaux, took a great interest in my well-being (so I was later informed), and naturally enquired about the whereabouts of my father. I have no knowledge of my mother's reply to that question, but I have learned of the desire of the Prideaux family, Marion in particular, to adopt me into their family.

At this time my mother had re-established contact with my absent father, but although a year had gone by since my arrival, she had not told him about me. Her reason for this reticence is unclear, but when Marion Prideaux became aware of this indiscretion, she insisted that my mother should write immediately and inform my father of his new responsibilities in the world.

Halfway through our time at Hamsell Lake House, a disagreement seems to have occurred between my mother and

Walter Prideaux, the husband of Marion. As a result, my mother was given notice to quit her post and move out forthwith. Desperate to reverse this situation, she turned for help to someone who would have sympathy and, above all, the verbal skills to reverse the decision.

Arthur Watson had married Lesley, my mother's friend and former flatmate, early in 1936. During their courtship he had met my mother several times and there was a great mutual respect between them. When the cry for assistance came through he did not hesitate, and made prompt arrangements to travel down to Hamsell House and meet the Prideaux by appointment.

Arthur was the quintessential English gentleman both in manner and attire, and was perfectly equipped to negotiate in a calm, reserved and factual way. After lengthy discussions, my mother's notice to quit was rescinded and things were returned to normality for a little while. However relationships between employer and employee had been damaged by this episode and in the late summer of 1948 we left the Prideaux family to seek pastures new.

A reference Marion Prideaux wrote for my mother in the early 1950s is very revealing:

I have known Doris Spencer since Norman was a baby. I am rather vague about dates – it must be around seven or eight years. Doris is a first class cook. At one time she had lessons at the Cordon Bleu in Sloane Street but she does simple things equally well.

I am not able to speak about housework as we were in a larger house than we are now when she was with us and she had not got housework to do. She is clean in person and in her work – though not always very tidy. She is thoroughly honest.

I can speak wholeheartedly for her kindness. The only warning I feel I ought to give is that she is a rather emotional person. She has had some hard knocks in her life and it is that perhaps that has made her extra sensitive.

In the years ahead some employers would take the last paragraph of the reference into consideration. Unfortunately they would be in the minority, and as a result, chaos would ensue.

Marion Prideaux never entirely severed her ties with my mother and she arranged to meet up with her on a couple of occasions at a location halfway between Eridge and New Romney. Sadly I have no memory of these meetings and only know that they did actually take place. Marion corresponded with my mother for a number of years afterwards. She would always enquire about my well-being, and often she would send a small quantity of money (usually a ten shilling note) with the instruction to place it in a savings account registered in my name. When, many years later, I came to read these correspondences, they revealed to me just how kind and considerate this lady was. In essence she was nothing less than my guardian angel in disguise.

One of my most treasured sentimental possessions is a small leather-bound Church of England book of common prayer. Inside the cover it bears the inscription:

To: Doris + Norman Peter
From W.T.P. M.F.P.
Nov. 25, 1946

The initials refer to Walter Treverbian Prideaux and Marion Fenn Prideaux.

After finally leaving the Prideaux household, my mother accepted a post as cook to Judge Alfred Frank Topham at their house near Yarmouth, Isle of Wight. After some seven months there the position was terminated and we returned to the mainland. Before leaving Yarmouth, Alice, the wife of Judge Topham, wrote a handwritten letter of reference for my mother. It read thus:

Cracknells
Yarmouth
Isle of Wight Tel. 240

To whom it may concern:
Mrs Spencer has been employed as a Cook General by me for a period of seven months, during which time I have found her honest + reliable, a nice cook and extremely quick in her work.
Her small son is very well behaved + a quiet child, he has been absolutely no trouble.
Alice Topham
March 10/49

It was early March 1949 and, for a brief while, we stayed in central London, in lodgings. During this time my step-grandmother up north wrote to my mother to suggest that she should seek employment back in the Barnard Castle area. However well-meaning this suggestion was, in reality it was not going to be that easy to find somewhere with accommodation for both of us.

It was not convenient for us to stay at my grandfather's house as he had become rather unwell and needed peace and quiet. Having a little boy living under the same roof, however quiet he might be, would have been impractical. To underline this situation I know that on October 10th 1951 my grandfather had travelled to Newcastle hospital for what was assumed to be a routine operation for an enlarged prostate gland. My step-grandmother Ethel accompanied him. After having an examination, he was informed that he had only about five days to live. This was of course a complete shock. He died on October 17th, but not before insisting that my mother should not be contacted about his condition. He felt it would have been a long and expensive journey for her to undertake and not a suitable time for a little boy to come.

Alas, I only have only a fleeting memory of my grandfather, from what must have been my first visit to his home at Stainton village near Barnard Castle. He made some wooden toys and bricks for me and painted them in bright colours.

Back to 1949. A couple of weeks passed by, and then we were off on our travels again. My mother had found employment as a cook at a residence near Canterbury in Kent. We would be there for one year before yet another change of job, this time to Seafield House in the coastal town of New Romney.

Mrs Prideaux was very concerned about these frequent moves, and wrote:

"Doris dear, I don't want to be hard, but I am distressed that you change places so often… I do so want you to be somewhere happy for you and Norman". In another letter she again voiced her concerns: "Dear Doris – you are having a hard time. I am sorry. I do hope that you will be able to go to a convalescent home with Norman until you have found a situation. I will let you know if I hear of anything".

New Romney was a very picturesque little town with a

miniature steam passenger railway. Trains ran daily along a coastal route to Hythe in one direction, Dungeness in the other. I have many pleasant childhood memories of journeys on this railway. The carriages were very basic with wooden seats and you were literally open to the elements. For a little boy it was a thrilling experience to have the wind, soot and steam blowing over your head as you travelled along listening all the time to the frantic rhythm of the miniaturised steam locomotive.

We had arrived in New Romney during March 1950, and some six months later, a milestone arrived which would be a stepping stone in every child's life. I had attained the age to attend school full-time.

Sadly I cannot recall anything at all about my first school, which maybe is not such a surprise. In the years ahead I would attend seven different primary schools and three secondary ones. Our time in Kent would last a mere two years, and from there on in the next three years we would live briefly at locations all over Southern England.

In March 1955 we arrived in Greatham, a village set deep in the heart of the Hampshire countryside. My mother had taken up the post of cook at the Manor House. This was the vast residence of Captain Augustus Coryton, his wife Violet and their three daughters, Caroline Julia, Sarah Jane and Lavinia Augusta Maude.

The village primary school I attended was just over half a mile away and thus within easy walking distance. The staff were very friendly and taught in a relaxed but very effective way. I quickly made new friends. The villagers themselves were as warm and unpretentious as the surrounding countryside.

Robert Smith, Victor Peters and a boy called Barney (his surname escapes me) and I formed a veritable quartet. We spent many happy hours together, fishing in the ponds and streams, roaming in the fields and heathland and looking for birds' nests in the many hedgerows. Sometimes we would simply enjoy our companionship up on the local hanger, the name given in Hampshire to a steeply-sided wooded hill. The hanger was a favourite haunt of ours and there we'd look for badger setts and rabbit warrens. Occasionally we'd discover a fossil or two from long ago or some other relic from the past.

One of my most treasured acquisitions was a badger's skull complete with a set of teeth. Needless to say, my mother was not impressed when I took it home to the Manor House!

There was never a time when we were bored. How could you be, when you were out in the clean country air living the dream of perfect freedom? Light pollution in the form of street lighting was practically non-existent and in the evening any traffic on the side roads was minimal. As a result, on clear evenings, the night sky glowed with the brilliance of the Milky Way and the stars of the solar system. Sometimes, if you looked upwards for long enough and were lucky, a shooting star would briefly appear. It made me think how insignificant our little planet was compared to what was shining in the heavens above.

I joined the local Cub Scouts Association, which met weekly at the nearby village of Liss. Afterwards there was usually time to buy some chips wrapped in newspaper and consume them while watching the trains bound for London or Portsmouth as they clickety-clacked past the level crossing gates. Although I was only nine, I felt I had become part of the local community, never thinking how fragile my place in all this really was.

The Manor House was an imposing building with its stables, smithy, walled courtyards, orchard, extensive lawns and kitchen gardens. From time to time members of the local foxhunt in all their regalia met in front of the house and the local blacksmith-farrier would carry out running repairs. As I watched him re-shoeing the horses I never ceased to wonder how they did not seem to feel any pain when a red-hot replacement shoe was held against a hoof in order to burn a suitable profile into it.

Our servants' quarters - two small bedrooms and a sitting room - were upstairs at the end of a long corridor in one of the annexes. The furniture, it has to be said, was very basic. Our only entertainment came from a radio in the main kitchen. Every week the BBC broadcast a half-hour science fiction programme called "Journey into Space" which had rapidly established cult status. My schoolpals had alerted me to it, and one evening a week I would spend my time listening to the bulky valve-driven radio receiver in its wooden cabinet.

My mother would be working away in the background preparing the evening meal for the Coryton family. The lady of the house would pay occasional visits to the kitchen to issue instructions to her and check on the progress of the meal she was preparing.

The Corytons liked to entertain and frequently held well-attended dinner parties. One evening I happened to be in the kitchen when one of these events was in progress. Halting her work momentarily, my mother beckoned me to come to the door opening onto the main hall and gently opened it a few inches. The noise made by the assembled guests all engaged in multi-conversations rose in a great crescendo.

"That's why God invented different languages - to stop idle chatter!" she exclaimed and then gently closed the door. Compared to the events playing out behind the door the kitchen was a haven of silence.

After a while it became clear to me that employer/employee

relationships were not always as affable as they should be. There were occasional fiery altercations between my mother and Violet Coryton. This should not have been such a surprise to me as they both had this edge to their personalities, which, when it surfaced, led to brief but energetic arguments. However this did not stop the Coryton family taking us with them on day trips to their friends' summer seaside house at West Wittering on the Selsey peninsular. The journey along the leafy Hampshire lanes took barely an hour. A picnic lunch would be unpacked on the almost deserted sandy beach, which had an exclusive feel to it, and the more adventurous would take a swim. These seaside visits are my last memories of seeing my mother in a bathing costume. She seemed to blend in with the Coryton family.

Behind the Manor House and gardens there was a vast field. It was bordered by a narrow copse which formed a natural boundary between the estate and Liss Forest Road. One summer's day in 1955 my friend Robert Smith and I had the bright idea of re-enacting a scene from a Wild West movie. Armed with a small axe, sheath knives and a bag containing jacket potatoes and butter, we walked across the field and found a suitable gap in the boundary fence. We were now inside the copse, which, in addition to the native trees, contained a large bamboo thicket. As cowboys do, we cut a small clearing, collected some dry wood and lit a campfire. With the heat rapidly rising, we laid the potatoes onto the glowing embers. We would soon be enjoying cooked potatoes Roy Rogers style.

But ill fortune was about to befall us. A swirling wind had suddenly developed and blown some sparks into the tinder-dry bamboo canes and foliage. Using some discarded branches, we desperately tried to snuff out the flames but it was no use. Within seconds the fire had grown into a spectacular wave of flames.

I can remember running across the field, my heart in my mouth, to where the Corytons were enjoying afternoon tea on the front lawn. Although I was somewhat breathless I still managed to blurt out, "The copse is alight! The copse is alight!"

It was hardly necessary for me to draw attention to this, as in the distance, flames and smoke were clearly visible to all. The local fire brigade was summoned and the fire quickly extinguished.

Now another kind of fire awaited Robert and me. After a brief questioning about our involvement in this incident, we were instructed to attend a meeting with Captain Coryton in his study at ten o'clock the following morning. By the time the following day had arrived the tension inside us had built up to an unbearable pitch.

We met up behind the Manor's outhouse block before entering the main building and approaching the study door. Knocking twice before the words "Enter" could be heard, we found ourselves standing before the Captain. An imposing framed painting of the Captain's father brandishing a shotgun loomed large behind him as he proceeded to question our reasons for setting the copse alight. Satisfied with our explanation, he emphasised that he would have to bear the cost of calling the fire brigade and hoped he would never again have to summon us to appear before him on such matters. We both promised this would not happen again and apologised profusely. Making a quick exit, we both agreed that it had been a chastening experience and one we never wanted to experience again. Roy Rogers and his cowhands' activities would, in future, be strictly limited to comics and movies!

Saturdays were usually my mother's day off, and we generally went by bus to the market town of Petersfield. After having lunch in an inexpensive café we would to go to the market and buy some sweets. Then it would be off to the cinema to view the latest film.

Occasionally my mother would have Sunday afternoon off as well as Saturday. If the weather was fine we would walk about a mile along Forest Road (which bordered the estate) and then ramble through the adjacent sandy heathland. There was an active single-track railway that had been driven through this landscape, and we used to sit on the high banking overlooking the line and enjoy a little picnic.

Sometimes a steam locomotive hauling several carriages would appear. There would never be a lack of passengers, as this was the Longmoor military railway, transporting soldiers in uniform. We would wave to them and they would, in turn, wave back. In the middle of the Hampshire countryside this was a surreal sight, and gave the feeling that the country was about to go to war again.

Towards the end of the summer a village fete would be held in the grounds of the Manor House, and for a while the entire population of Greatham would seem to have gathered there. I quickly learnt that stalls advertising "a prize every time" did not mean that every entrant won. Maybe the present day high-powered surreptitious advertising formats owe their roots to such village fetes held deep in the English countryside!

On Saturday October 15th 1955, a great event was celebrated. The eldest of the Coryton daughters, Caroline Julia, had been married at Greatham Baptist Church earlier in the day and now a grand reception was being held at the Manor House. Extra help had been drafted in and I can vividly remember the scene in the kitchen where my mother was working hard preparing food (and doing a little complaining about the extra pressure to meet a tight deadline). Cars seemed to be arriving every minute, and the kitchen door was constantly opening and shutting as refreshments were ferried to the main hall and the living rooms. This was the very first time I had ever tasted champagne, and although it was probably of the highest quality, I had no desire to repeat the experience!

A large crowd gathered at the main entrance to see the happy couple off. Being uninterested in all the gabble of noise, I remained in the kitchen. Once the roar of an expensive car and the sound of tin cans attached by string dragging along the gravel driveway had subsided, normality returned.

For a short while our lives at the Manor House were on an even keel, although the kitchen-based altercations between my mother and Mrs Coryton would occasionally surface. Like a passing thunderstorm, these would last but a few minutes, and were almost a normal part of life there.

Christmas 1955 came and went and spring was here again. Our time in Hampshire continued without event until the New Year of 1957 arrived. With it came notice for my mother to leave the Corytons' employment. She took me to see the headmistress at the primary school to explain to her why I would be leaving the school. The walk back to the Manor House must have been traumatic for her, as I cried all the way and kept saying over and over again "Mum, I don't want to leave. Why can't we stay here?" It was to no avail, and I had to say goodbye to my friends and the good times we had enjoyed together. My time in this part of Hampshire had been tranquil and idyllic, a wonderful experience and one I will never forget.

In the years that followed, Captain Coryton gradually became an alcoholic and drank away the family fortune before eventually having to move into more modest accommodation a couple of miles away from the Manor House. Many years later, during a telephone conversation, Julia Fisher, née Coryton, would recall me as having been a "very precocious child". The Manor House was eventually sold to the L'Abri Foundation, which owns it to the present day. The days of high-society living there have gone forever.

Our departure in January 1957 from the Manor House saw a move to the town of Cobham in Surrey. This was the home of city accountant Mr Roy Jones. Once more it was time to attend a new school, make new friends and move forward. My mother continued to portray herself as a war widow, and I developed the impression that my father had perished in the war. At the age of 11, with all the post-war propaganda in the media, I naturally assumed that the Germans were responsible for his demise.

Mr Jones was from the United States, and for a time the situation was one of harmony, until his pregnant wife had a miscarriage. He descended into depression over this unfortunate event and decided to dispense with my mother's services.

Fortunately, if you can call it that, this latest termination of employment took place in July 1957, which meant that my education was at the changeover stage between primary and secondary school. On the 27th of March I had taken, and subsequently failed to pass, the eleven-plus examination which would determine if you were to attend grammar school or secondary school. This was a desperate disappointment for me, as the difference between the two systems of education was a determining factor in one's future prospects of employment.

The headmaster at Cobham primary school had called me to one side to gently inform me of my failure, which was, he said, due to a poor mark in mathematics. During my brief time at this school I had achieved second place in a class of 47, and can only think that on the day of the exam nerves had got the better of me.

All in all my education would go on to span attendance at 10 different primary and secondary schools in Kent, Sussex, Wiltshire, Hampshire, Surrey, Huntingdonshire and Essex. Initially all these moves did not appear to seriously affect my academic progress, but inevitably the lack of continuity and consistency took its toll over the long term. It would really catch up with me in my final three years, between the ages of 12 and 15.

Our frequent migrations affected my life in other ways, too. During all this time of nomadic existence my mother and I had been able to visit her good friend Lesley Watson two or three times a year. Her home in the south-eastern London suburb of Honor Oak Park was a neat terraced house where she lived with her husband Arthur and their three sons Chester, Barry and Tony. For my mother these visits were a welcome escape from a harsh, unforgiving world, and she and Lesley would spend many happy hours reminiscing about their pre-war times together.

Back then the two young women often met up after work for a chat, usually at a Lyons Corner House, a well-known chain of teashops at that time. When the time of each visit had come to an end we would make our way round the corner to Honor Oak Park railway station. Descending down the steep stairways to the platform we would wait for our train to London Bridge. We always glanced across the line towards the row of terraced houses above the opposite embankment. There, from their upstairs window, the Watsons could be seen waving goodbye to us.

Having left Cobham, my mother took up a temporary appointment at a large country house near the county town of

Hertford, Hertfordshire. It was a depressing sort of place and our accommodation, separate from the house, resembled a converted horse-stable! I was not sorry when my mother applied for and got a more permanent position at Didgemere Hall, the home of the Nicholls family in the village of Roydon, Essex.

CHAPTER THREE

LEAVING SCHOOL

Our arrival at Roydon in the summer of 1957 would coincide with the beginning of my education at secondary (high) school. This is a landmark event in any child's educational experience, and so it was for me.

It was a bright, sunny early September morning when I walked with my mother down the lane from Didgemere Hall to the top village green, where other new pupils had congregated. We waited for the school bus to appear and transport us to our newly-constructed school in nearby Harlow New Town. This was the first day of official occupancy for Potter Street (Technical and Modern) Secondary School, and we were all filled with expectation and a little anxiety for a new era in our lives.

After collecting other pupils at various stops along the way, we finally arrived at our brand-new, gleaming school with its modern state-of-the art buildings and hastily-completed unfenced playgrounds. In later years, until it closed in 2008, it would be renamed Brays Grove Community College. As testament to the quality of this institution, it appointed a mere three heads of school during the entire 51 years of its existence.

Alas, after I had attended the school for a very happy 20 months, my mother's employment was again terminated, and I had to inform the Headmaster, Sydney Bottoms, that I was leaving. On my last day he called me into his office and tried to allay my obvious distress at having to leave. He handed me a letter addressed to my mother.

My journey home on the school bus that day was desperately gloomy and I did my best not to cry in front of my schoolfriends. I made sure I succeeded, for this was an era when boys were not supposed to cry in public.

After handing my mother the letter from the headmaster I eventually got to read the brief contents. At the end of the text Mr Bottoms had written the phrase "I gave Norman some fatherly advice". Such advice was all too often in short supply, and in this instance it came from a man who was truly a great headmaster. I had loved my time at this school and looked forward to every day spent there, as did all the other pupils.

During all this experience I had begun to form an idea of my future career; I wanted to become a radio and television engineer. On my penultimate day in Roydon I went to see Alan Coles, who had become one of my best friends in the village. I told him my new address and said that I hoped to get back to see him some time in the future.

Small in stature but big-hearted and loyal, Alan was in my eyes a quality person. I felt shot to pieces at having to say goodbye to him.

"We're all going to miss you, Norman" he said. These were Alan's parting words to me. Although we corresponded for a time, our paths were destined never to cross again.

When my mother and I left Roydon it was to move to another part of Essex, some 20 miles away. Holfield Grange was a large, rambling country mansion owned by Colonel Francis Hill, some two miles from the pretty town of Coggeshall. This then was our new location (I hesitate to use the word home) and I was duly enlisted to attend the local secondary school. This institution was to be a real culture shock and there was a great contrast between it and the one I had had to leave behind in Harlow New Town.

The main building was a fine red brick structure, but it had outgrown its capacity and was supplemented by several prefabricated buildings. The school canteen doubled up as a sports changing room and had a real air of decay about it. This and a lack of modern facilities handicapped the teaching staff there, some of whom had an attitude more akin to the 1940s than the 1960s.

This new experience was initially a cruel disappointment, but from my mother I had learned that you had to make the best of a bad job and soldier on – there was really no point in feeling sorry for yourself. As the weeks passed my disconsolate mood began to improve and I became more integrated into the everyday life of the school and the social interaction outside it.

I remember some of my new schoolpals persuading me to come with them one Saturday on a trip to Colchester on the local service bus. They were all going to attend a professional football match at Layer Road, where the local team, Colchester United, were due to play against East Anglian rivals Norwich City. I had never been to a professional football match before this and wondered what all the fuss was about.

I soon found out when Colchester scored after 24 seconds! Pandemonium ensued for several minutes before things settled down to normal, though I had seen little of the early action. The problem was that the ground was packed with 15,000 fans and

I had found my view obstructed. I could only see the backs of people's heads and many waving arms. To make matters worse, most of those obstructing my view were Norwich fans!

Rather than dampen my enthusiasm, this experience heightened it. In the weeks that passed, I attended as many home games as I could and even some reserve fixtures. I had found a place where I could go and enjoy a couple of hours' entertainment and find some escape from a bleak, unforgiving world.

Saturdays were usually the only day off work for my mother, and we used to make a point of getting away from the Grange on this day. We would walk the half-mile down the lane to the main road and catch a bus to either Colchester or Braintree. Once there we would do some window shopping before having lunch in an inexpensive café. Then it would be on to the cinema or, if Colchester United were playing at home, I would go to the match and meet my mother afterwards.

When in Colchester a visit to Marks the Tailor in St John Street was a regular event. The shop interior had a split level. The high level was designated for bespoke tailoring, the lower for the latest fashion in men's casual clothing. Mr and Mrs Marks were always in attendance, and for some reason they always showed an interest in my welfare and enquired how I was progressing in my education. I told them that the subject of mathematics was causing me some difficulties, and they suggested that I might benefit from some additional private tuition. The reality was that the cost of this would have been unaffordable for my mother.

She and Mrs Marks used to hold long conversations. The topics were usually the world in general and what to do to put it to rights. It was almost as if they had known each other all their lives.

While all this was going on I would be surveying the items on display. On some occasions I had saved enough money from my paper round to be able to buy a nice tie or shirt. However this was a very rare event, and most times I could only stand and admire what lay in front of me. I had a secret dream in which one day I would actually walk out of the shop wearing all the latest trendy gear. It was, however, only a dream. Back in those times the lifestyle in rural Essex was less complicated than today, though that is not to say it was ever easier. The expectations in life were more basic, and in some respects more contented than today.

The school term ended in December 1960. I had already passed the age of 15, so it was time for me to leave and seek employment.

The next few weeks brought a new set of problems and challenges. I had made several applications for an apprenticeship in the electrical/radio and television trades without success. As if to add to this continued disappointment, the prospect of another upheaval surfaced when Colonel Hill's wife Judith decided to terminate my mother's employment. In no time at all our few possessions were being loaded up and transported to the house of my mother's new employer. This was at Lexden, near Colchester, the residence of Sir Tom Hickinbotham.

Soon after our arrival here the youth employment authorities, who had been monitoring my employment searches, suggested that it would be prudent for me to return to education at nearby Stanway Secondary School. I readily agreed to do this and found Stanway to be a wonderful school, but found that I was trailing behind my fellow classmates. I persevered and began to make progress until, out of the blue, my mother was once again given notice to quit. In the end Sir Tom had turned out to be a rather unpleasant person. He had once been the Governor of Aden, and he behaved as if he still was.

Once more we were on our way to another destination. There were to be three more in as many months, together with a weekend at a Colchester hostel.

As luck would have it, my mother eventually secured a more permanent appointment back in one of our original areas. It came to pass that we arrived back in Coggeshall, at a large Elizabethan farmhouse known as Scrip's Farm. This was the residence of Lady Binney.

I had concealed these domestic upheavals from my classmates in order not to appear inferior. There is little doubt that it was affecting my academic performance.

We seemed to be getting established at Scrip's Farm when the time came for me to leave Stanway School and make another attempt to find employment. The headmaster had urged me to stay on, but I felt that the overwhelming desire to become a breadwinner was simply too much.

Once again I trawled the local employers looking for an apprenticeship, and once again, after a few interviews and applications, I came up with nothing. I was just 15 years old with no academic qualifications and no family home. To an outside observer, I had no future prospects. My personal outlook was always one of hope, though this was being challenged with every rejection.

This was particularly hurtful when I went along for an interview at a Braintree television dealer's shop. The owner sat me down and asked the usual round of probing questions, which I thought I had answered to the best of my ability. "Please come back on Monday, then I will tell you if you have been successful," he said. I went away feeling happy to be told that.

Monday came and I arrived at the shop. I went to the counter and explained that I had come to see the owner for a reply about a job application. Moments later he appeared at the top of the stairs which led to the repair workshop. "Sorry lad – I don't think it would work out," he said. "Goodbye. " He called this out without even bothering to come down the stairs to face me. I left the premises with my heart in my boots.

Later, the local youth employment agency, having sent me there and seen my dilemma, suggested that for the time being I should look for a less skilled occupation. I could still look for an apprenticeship whist being gainfully in employment.

I applied for and accepted the post of junior factory floor assistant at the local factory of Swinbornes', manufacturers of isinglass and gelatine. Although my tasks there did not require a great deal of skill, at least it was a start, and Swinbornes' was a stable secure company to work for. However stability and security had never been part of our world, and sure enough, after a time the news broke that Lady Binney no longer required my mother's services. Once again we were off on our travels, with the additional consequence that I had to quit my job at the factory.

Although my tasks there had been fairly basic ones the company managing director called me into his office on my last day and wished me well for the future. This was a nice gesture from a true gentleman.

The future was to be in the next county, Suffolk, at the home of Major James Campbell and his wife Violet. My mother went to be interviewed at their home near the village of Benhall, and I accompanied her on a somewhat tortuous journey by bus. It took over two hours of travelling before we eventually got to meet Mrs Campbell. She spoke first with my mother, and after being satisfied that she was suitable for the post she asked what kind of job I would be looking for in Suffolk. I duly told her of my hopes for an apprenticeship in the electrical trade and she seemed suitably impressed.

Mrs Campbell seemed to be a nice person, and with the interview completed we travelled back to Coggeshall in good spirits. However I did not really want to be leaving Essex. The main part of my education had been spent there, and the good memories far outweighed some of the bad ones.

Leaving Scrip's Farm and the town of Coggeshall was not a pleasant experience. I have a very vivid memory of all our worldly possessions being unloaded from the taxi and taken up onto the platform at Kelvedon railway station, in readiness for the arrival of the train to Saxmundham, Suffolk.

Kelvedon station has elevated platforms, and on this particular day the prevailing wind was blowing across the Spartan facilities with a vengeance. Sitting on one of our much-travelled and somewhat battered luggage trunks, braving the elements, I had the overwhelming feeling of being a refugee who did not really know where he was going and was more than a little fearful of what lay ahead.

It was almost as if a scene in a drama documentary was being played out. But this was no rehearsal - it was for real.

CHAPTER FOUR

A PUZZLING DISCOVERY

Our train journey from Kelvedon involved changing trains at Colchester and Ipswich. On each occasion the guard would unload our old battered luggage trunk and suitcase onto the platform ready for transfer. Finally we reached Saxmundham.

Our arrival in Suffolk didn't augur well at all for our future there. My mother's new employers, Major James Campbell and his wife Violet, met us at the railway station and the station porter loaded all our worldly possessions onto their estate car. Just as we were about to move off my mother asked: "I gave the porter two-and-six tip - was that enough?" The Major answered, "We don't give that kind of money away here in Saxmundham" Already I felt trepidation about what lay ahead.

We were driven to their family home, a large meandering country mansion set off a narrow lane near the tiny village of Benhall. Initially my fears seemed unfounded. Being a lady with some influence in the local community, Mrs Campbell had arranged for me to attend an interview with a local electrical company, G A Hubbard and Son Ltd of Saxmundham. They were situated only two miles from the Campbells' house, so I could get there easily by bicycle.

Shortly after my interview a letter arrived informing me that my application for employment had been successful and they would be willing to employ me as a first-year apprentice. I would begin by working at their Saxmundham electrical workshop.

Hubbards sent all their apprentices to college one day a week for technical training. This system was termed "day release", but it had not initially been included in my offer of employment. When I told Mrs Campbell this, she immediately summoned the county youth employment officer to travel up from Ipswich for a meeting at Benhall. She had clearly used her influence because, to my surprise, he responded to her demand and came up to Benhall to interview me.

I think he must have sensed that although my education had been severely disrupted, my enthusiasm to learn was never in doubt. In any event he told me that he thought I would benefit greatly from part-time day attendance at college and would give his recommendation to Hubbards. True to his word, on my first day at Hubbards they gave me details of how to enrol on a part-time day release course at Ipswich Civic College. The 'day release' agreement would require me to attend the college for one day and one evening every week. In order to simplify this the college had scheduled the two required attendances to take place on the same day. Lectures and workshop practice would commence at 9 am. These would continue, with breaks, until 9 pm. Combined with the 44-mile round trip by train, it meant this would be a very long day, but nevertheless an interesting one.

At Hubbards, it really was a case of starting at the bottom of the ladder. I was set to work at a corner bench in the electrical workshop. There I assisted an electrician called Bob, whose job was to repair and recondition automobile starter motors and generators. Elsewhere in the workshop other electricians were working on domestic appliance repairs, motor rewinding and, in a separated section, lead acid battery restoration. In the same building there was an electrical storeroom with a separate entrance and counter, where two storekeepers, Joe Elmy and Algy (whose surname I cannot recall), operated an efficient inventory.

Joe, 53, tall and bespectacled with wiry hair, had only recently given up playing football in the local league. He was an extremely affable character who made me feel welcome. As the senior storekeeper at Hubbards, he ran the unit with iron efficiency. If there had been a vacancy going for President of the World, I am sure Joe would have filled it with equal zest!

Adjacent to the stores counter was a small office. This was the base of the company electrical foreman Richard (Dick) Mogridge. Dick would estimate costs of customers' requests, purchase materials and organise the manpower for the relevant contract work.

A few yards away from the main workshop lay another prefabricated building which housed the television and radio repair department, with a staff of 10 engineers. The retail shop and television showroom was a short distance away, down a slope in Market Place.

After some time settling in working in the repair workshop, I had begun to note the activities of the electrical installation crew. This part of Hubbards' operations consisted of a fleet of around eight vans with an electrician and an apprentice assigned to each vehicle. The crews, known as the 'outside staff', would leave the depot each morning to travel to their various contacts and assignments in the surrounding district. From talking to my fellow apprentices, I managed to gain an insight into the type of work, skills and locations which made up their working day. It all seemed far more interesting, and indeed challenging, than my daily assignments. Each morning as the crews sped off, I would envy them. I could only bide my time.

Eventually, when I had built up some confidence and experience, I politely asked if I might be transferred to work with the installation crew. To my surprise and delight, my wish was granted. Although at first some of the work was fairly basic and physical, it meant that I was able to escape the confines of the depot and see more of the outlying villages and towns. This new situation meant that I would be working in many different shops, farms, factories and houses.

On one occasion I found myself directed to the private residence of the head of the firm, Geoffrey Ambrose Hubbard. When conversing between themselves employees would refer to him as "Geoff Hubbard", but whenever they had to meet him in person he was addressed as "Mr Hubbard". He had recently sold off the controlling interest of the company for a not inconsiderable sum while at the same time retaining a position on the board of directors. With the proceeds of this transaction (£66,000) he had purchased an Elizabethan manor house. Out in the extensive grounds were a number of outhouse buildings which were being used to house a herd of pigs.

On our arrival in a company van, Mr Hubbard had suddenly appeared. Dressed in casual country clothes and wellington boots, he began to walk towards the vehicle. He was carrying two laden buckets which I presumed contained some form of liquid feed for his burgeoning stock of animals.

One of the electricians, the ever rebellious Mick, who was safely out of earshot inside the van, commented, "Just look at that silly old ******, you'd never think he was worth £66,000". In today's terms that would be around £ 1. 5 million.

Mr Hubbard had now reached our van. Mick wound the window down to speak. "Good morning, Mr Hubbard" he said. "We've brought the boy for you. "

I got out of the van carrying my toolkit and a cardboard box containing the materials required. Mr Hubbard handed me a list of the tasks to completed by the end of the working day. My workmates prepared to depart and gave me some final instructions. "Listen boy" said Mick (apprentices were all called 'boy' back then to leave them in no doubt of their lowly status), "When we return at 4. 30, make sure you've finished and are ready to go. If you aren't, you can walk home". Which was a distance of seventeen miles.

I have never worked so hard in a single day. My fellow apprentices felt that the joke was on me, as nobody really wanted to work at Geoff Hubbard's home, with all the possible consequences if anything went wrong. Fortunately I survived and Mr Hubbard seemed to be satisfied with the work I had done. I completed the work on time and didn't have to walk the seventeen miles home!

Working for a well-known local company was not very rewarding financially, but it did give me the chance to experience working on various domestic, commercial and industrial projects. It also gave me the opportunity to see different areas of Suffolk.

My mother's situation was far from ideal. The fact that the Campbell's home was so remote made it difficult, indeed virtually impossible, for her to meet people. It was certainly a far cry from her days in London in the 1930s and 40s. It didn't help that the locals themselves were not exactly welcoming towards strangers. Indeed there was a saying that you had to live in Suffolk for 10 years before you were accepted. In addition my mother was finding it hard to cope with the sheer physical demands of her work, and she often felt unwell.

We had arrived in Benhall during the late summer of 1961. In the springtime of '62, without warning, Mrs Campbell gave my mother notice to quit. We were told to leave by the end of the month. My mother wrote to Massey's Agency in London to see if they had any vacancies for a cook in the Saxmundham area. There were none, and the market for domestic servants was flat. A frantic search elsewhere yielded nothing. Mrs Campbell, seeing this situation unfolding before her, made some alternative enquiries.

She came to say that she did not want to see us become homeless and had come up with a "solution". She had provisionally arranged for my mother to move into a hostel provided for single women. I was to be put into a hostel run by the Salvation Army.

I listened to Mrs Campbell's words in sheer disbelief. Once more I felt like a refugee in the land of my birth. If ever a father figure was required, this was the moment. But any such person still remained hidden in the shadows.

To this day I do not know exactly what went wrong between my mother and Mrs Campbell. From being at the outset a friendly and helpful person, Mrs Campbell had morphed into some kind of villainess. We were now placed in an impossible situation with nowhere to go and no one able, or willing, to help.

In the early sixties the Social Services Department gave little or no assistance to someone classed as a single woman. Nevertheless, in desperation, my mother contacted them and they arranged for us to attend an interview at their Saxmundham offices. We were ushered into a room where a moustached man in a tweed suit listened to my mother describe our plight. He didn't ponder long. He could, he said, offer us some form of accommodation almost immediately. Before either of us could register any sense of relief, he added "in Birmingham".

I was completely stunned by this statement. I was not normally given to challenging authority at the age of seventeen, but this was the moment to overcome my deference. I asked the social worker how he thought I could continue to work as an apprentice electrician in Saxmundham while living in a city a hundred and eighty miles away.

His reply couldn't have been simpler. It was, he said, extremely unlikely that I would be offered further employment by Hubbards when I reached the end of my apprenticeship. There was no suitable accommodation available in the area. Therefore his proposal offered us much greater security, and we would be wise to accept it.

This response was not only unhelpful, it made me feel utterly degraded. I could sense my valued apprenticeship slipping away from me. In just one sentence, this man had made both of us feel wretched. Now it was very clear that we were the only people who could help ourselves.

Some of my workmates had by now heard about my predicament, and one of them innocently asked me what I was going to do. Would I be leaving to go and live in Birmingham? I choked up, unable to reply.

With the deadline for our stay at the Campbells' fast approaching, I confided our situation to a friend who lived in Benhall village. Terry Gunton and I had a good friendship and we were both enthusiasts of the game of football. Like myself, he was an apprentice, learning the bricklaying trade. After completing his apprenticeship Terry would eventually go on to become self-employed and build some 50 houses in and around the village of Wenhaston.

Terry took me to meet his parents at their bungalow to see if they could help us in our plight. They had come to Benhall from Norfolk and lived in a nice bungalow. After listening to the story, they promised to look out for any vacant furnished accommodation in the area.

Unfortunately this type of accommodation was already at a premium in the area. I could see by the expression on the faces of Terry's parents that they felt the situation was grim. The high influx of temporary workers at the Sizewell Nuclear Power Station construction site had swallowed up all such accommodation.

The days ticked by with no sign of an answer to our predicament. As usual my mother was putting forward a brave face on things, but I was feeling an increasing and overwhelming sense of despair. The world around me just did not seem to be fair at all.

Just as all seemed hopeless, my mother managed to secure some furnished accommodation at a nearby village. Now I could keep my highly-prized job while she could look for employment to help pay the rent and buy our food. It seemed the sun had at last shone down on us. I was able to continue to enjoy my weekly day release attendance at Ipswich College. There I was meeting other apprentices and learning new skills. I used to spend a good part of every weekend studying so that I could make a good attempt of the course homework. My disrupted schooldays were coming back to bite me!

In Aldringham our furnished accommodation could only be described as basic. It was at the home of a retired surveyor and his wife, and he was not a very affable man. I remember coming home one evening to find him chastising my mother for leaving a light on, thus using too much of his electricity. Shortly after this incident he informed her that his wife's sister was coming to live there. We were given until the end of the month to move out. Once again the threat of homelessness was staring us in the face.

After a worrying few days, my mother came up with a masterstroke: a caravan on a site in the nearby town of Leiston had become available to rent. With my wages, small as they were, and her earnings from a part-time cleaning job we could just about afford it. Now we were able to move out of the surveyor's house to somewhere more secure.

The caravan was 18' x 9' and around 15 years old. It was sited on pitch 13! It had a tiny galley kitchen and one single room 12' x 9'. At night-time a folding partition converted this space into two compact bedrooms. A solid fuel stove provided the main source of heating. If nothing else our new home was cosy, and it provided us with a degree of security. This was something my mother had never enjoyed as long as she was in service. Provided we managed to pay the rent on time and did not infringe the site rules, we were safe from the whims of any employer. That little caravan was to be our lifeline for the next 10 years.

St George's Caravan park stood in a large open area half a mile from the town centre. There were 90 caravans which, although having concrete paths outside them, had no hard-standing pitch. In the centre of the park a communal building housed showers, toilets and a washing machine annexe. There was no direct mains water supply to the individual pitches – you had to collect your domestic needs in a carboy from the communal amenities building. Mains drainage was not present either, so a soakaway had to be dug for the disposal of washing-up water. Electricity was restricted to a 5 amp supply which was only sufficient to power a few low wattage lamps, a television or radio and a small domestic iron. Cooking was done on a gas stove fed from a portable Propane gas bottle.

Most of the residents living on the park were working at the nearby Sizewell construction site. They had come from other parts of the UK, bringing with them their own family-sized caravans. The attraction was the high wage levels and overtime at Sizewell. The high skill demand greatly exceeded the local supply, so many of these people were civil, mechanical and electrical engineers, tradesmen and architects.

On completion Sizewell would be the most powerful nuclear power station in the world. Previously there had been only a little fishing village on this part of the Suffolk coast. At the peak of construction 2,000 people worked on site there. In 1961 the nearby town of Leiston had a population of only 4,111, so the impact on the local area and its economy was enormous. I would spend a lot of my free time studying my college work, riding around on my cycle or going to the beach only two miles away. Sometimes I would collect driftwood to burn in our stove. There was a never-ending supply being washed ashore, and it cost nothing. The gentle, rolling Suffolk landscape around Leiston always made the sky appear vast. It seemed to emphasise the rural isolation of the locality.

Compared with today's consumer world they were very unsophisticated times. We and many other people had very little, but we never yearned for extravagant material things.

At college I had become friendly with two other apprentice electricians. Danny May and Anthony Lawes were working for

Taylor Woodrow Construction at the Sizewell site. They always made it clear to me that although their working week was much longer than mine, their pay-packet was very much higher. Added to this was the status of working on such an important and massive construction site. The work at Hubbards was consistent, but being on the power station site seemed to put you in another league, both technically and financially.

Although living in the caravan represented a great step forward in terms of security, I wanted to buy it rather than continue renting. Then it really would be ours. I asked Brian Wright, the site warden, if he would contact the hire company to see if they would be willing to sell.

Brian came back with the news that the asking price would be £75. This sum far exceeded any meagre savings we had, so I had to tell him that it was beyond my reach. Seeing my predicament, he promised to go back to the company and see if they would lower the price. He was as good as his word, for in a short while, an offer to sell at £50 came through. To ease the burden they would allow it to be paid in twelve monthly instalments.

For once someone was being considerate towards us, and I felt a debt of gratitude towards Brian Wright for helping negotiate the purchase. My mother had found a part-time cleaning job at the power station, which was just a short bus ride from the caravan site. It all helped to supplement our modest income and also gave her an opportunity to meet other people. This was important for her, as life on a caravan site can be lonely.

From time to time I would hear brief accounts of her time in work, and sometimes one or two names of people would come to the fore. One such person was "Canadian Mike", who was deemed to be a very likeable and funny man. I never had a chance to meet Canadian Mike and only briefly wondered why my mother seemed to like him so much. Maybe it was the transatlantic accent. In the event the cleaning job only lasted for a few weeks, but at least my mother had been able to get out and mix with other people.

We were sitting watching television together one Friday evening when suddenly the scheduled programme was interrupted. An announcer I had never seen before then appeared on the screen. There had, he said, been an "incident" in Dallas, Texas, involving President Kennedy. The President had been wounded. When we heard that, everything seemed to stand still.

The announcer went off-screen and a logo in the form of a spinning globe replaced him. After several minutes he reappeared and began to repeat the previous information.

Suddenly a telephone on his desk rang. Lifting the receiver, he took a brief message, replaced it and looked straight ahead. He then made the sombre announcement: "We regret to announce that President Kennedy is dead".

Once more the spinning globe reappeared, amid an eerie silence. My mother and I sat stunned for a few minutes unable to absorb the enormity of what had happened. It seemed like optimism in America and the world also died that evening. It was of course November 22nd 1963.

This landmark event had taken place at a time of rapid changes in British society. After a slow start, a real shift away from post-war attitudes and conventions now began to gather pace. The "beat generation" had emerged, bringing with it an explosion of rock and pop music, flamboyant clothes and new words. This new era tended to be most influential in London and the provincial cities of Liverpool and Manchester. In the words of Bob Dylan, "The Times They Are a-Changin'".

Living where I was within throwing distance of the wild Suffolk coast meant that a lot of these new influences were slower in making their presence felt. Nonetheless I found myself enthralled with the new music, even though the opportunity to hear it was restricted to a few radio and television programmes.

I was delighted when, in March 1964, popular music began to be broadcast from a ship moored off the Essex coast. Radio Caroline was now transmitting it 24 hours a day, and the reception of it in Leiston was good. In fact it was teenage heaven!

Winter came and went, but my interest in the power station did not wane. Hubbards had experienced a downturn in work, and I found myself being alternated between Saxmundham and the Leiston and Aldeburgh branches of the firm. It didn't seem as secure as before.

My college friends urged me to write to Taylor Woodrow and ask if they would consider taking on another apprentice electrician at Sizewell. Encouraged by this, I wrote off. In the letter I told of my association with their two apprentices and enclosed a copy of a recent college report. I knew that, if asked, Danny and Tony would both present a good account of me. A reply came back asking me to attend an interview with their Chief Electrical Engineer, Mr Les Birgelem, on Monday June 22nd 1964.

I have no doubt that had Hubbards come to know of my intentions back then, they would have summarily dismissed me on the grounds of disloyalty. After all, they had been paying for me to attend college with the long-term view of obtaining a return for their initial investment. This distinct possibility made me feel very uneasy about my forthcoming interview.

I needed some peace of mind over this, so I sought and got an assurance from Taylor Woodrow that they wouldn't tell

Hubbards of my application should I not be offered a job. It was an unconventional thing to do, but the very thought of losing my apprenticeship altogether really tested my nerve. All in all it was a massive gamble, but the prospect of improving myself proved irresistible.

The interview with Mr Birgelem seemed to take place in a blur. It was all over in around 10 minutes flat. The usual pattern of things was reversed; he left the room first, hurriedly saying as he did so that he thought that I was looking for experience and that I would receive an offer very shortly.

The following week seemed an eternity, but sure enough, a letter arrived offering me an apprenticeship. The letter stipulated that I would be based at Sizewell for one year. After that I would be afforded the option of either being transferred to the permanent staff at the power station or moving to another Taylor Woodrow site. At last the future looked infinitely brighter, and I felt a deep gratitude towards my college friends at the power station for all their help and advice.

During my final few days of employment at Hubbards, Richard Mogridge approached me and wished me well. He said that, in his view, I had made the right decision for my future. It was a nice gesture, and it came from someone who was an important member of Hubbards' staff. I'll never forget just how much his brief few words enhanced my self-esteem at this time of transition.

My mother's situation still left much to be desired. She had found a part-time job as a cleaner at a local engineering works which involved two separate shifts each day. There was no direct public transport from the caravan park to the factory, so she had to trudge back and forth in all weathers. I was painfully aware that she was finding this a real struggle, even though she put a brave face on it. I knew my next goal in life would be to earn enough to support us both. Then it would no longer be necessary for her to do this type of work.

One evening we decided that the cupboards in the caravan needed reorganising. I set upon this task with a will, determined to get it out of the way before my favourite TV programme came on. After a few minutes I came across a bundle of old letters. As time was running out, I only cursorily ran my eye over the last few lines of a letter. It was signed "Joe" and the tone was affectionate.

"Who's Joe?" I asked.

"Joe? Oh, he was an American I knew during the war... Give me those, please!" my mother asked firmly but politely. I handed them to her and she put them away somewhere. I thought no more about them.

It never occurred to me that there might be some connection between this reaction and her response to other questions I'd posed some months before. Surely, I'd thought, if my father's been killed on active service in the war, my mother was entitled to draw a war widow's pension. However paltry, it could have made a real difference. Whereas, as a boy, I'd never asked about him, now that I was in my late teens I was becoming a bit more curious about the father I'd never known. So I asked where he'd been killed and whether he had a grave somewhere. All I got by way of an answer was: "Oh, don't bother me with questions like that now!" And that was that.

It wasn't something I dwelt too much on, but I was aware of feeling more vulnerable in situations which might require some fatherly support. I did have a sense that at some time or other in my mother's life she had experienced something traumatic of which she did not want to be reminded. I did not feel it was my place to press her further about this. My mother wasn't alone in being reluctant to talk about her feelings. We lived in a world where having reluctance to open up to others about painful personal experiences was deemed normal behaviour. In any event, back then your parents' word was always respected and rarely, if ever, challenged directly.

The assumption that my father had perished, presumably at the hands of the German military, had left me with a mixture of disappointment and covert anger. Occasionally this anger would surface. One of the most notable instances took place when we were living in the quiet leafy village of Kingswood, Surrey. The year was 1954 and I was nine years old. My mother was now cook in a large house in a good residential part of the village. I'd been told by schoolfriends that a very distinctive blond boy who lived a few streets away was German, and whenever I caught sight of him on his bicycle I'd shout out, "Go home to Germany, you killed my father!" Always, on hearing my cry, he would cycle away from me at speed with his head bowed. In my own way I was trying to get even with the people who had perpetrated such a terrible crime against my mother and me. At the age of nine this was my only opportunity to express my inherent anger and reveal my conscious interest in my father.

As an adult I'm ashamed of my behaviour regarding this, and realise how easy it is to jump to conclusions about individuals and peoples. This is particularly applicable when your knowledge is purely based on crude stereotypes and inherent prejudice. At the time I little thought that one day I'd have good friends in Germany, and delight in visiting that country many times.

Some good news came through from Ipswich College. I had successfully passed my first City and Guilds diploma examination. I felt a great satisfaction at this minor achievement.

It was a proud day for me when I presented myself at the Sizewell site as a new Taylor Woodrow employee. Everyone was very welcoming, though my subsequent introduction to the Foreman Electrician ensured that I did not automatically think I had "made it".

I was taken into his office to meet him. "Good morning, Norman" he said. "My name is Bill Weaver. Everyone here calls me Mike. You can call me Mike too, but remember, I'll still sack you!" For a shy, nervous 18-year-old on his very first day in a new job, this was even more unnerving.

To counteract this experience a letter from the college arrived at our caravan to help raise my self-esteem. I had acquired the additional accolade of being awarded the course prize for 1963/64. My new employers were suitably impressed by this and sent me a congratulatory note.

There were now three apprentice electricians working for Taylor Woodrow on the power station site, Daniel May, Anthony Lawes and I. We all loved our jobs and wanted to stay with the company when the construction contract was completed, and we constantly speculated where our next destination would be.

These were formative and stimulating times for us. We worked three weekends a month as extra overtime, but the work was interesting and enjoyable, so it wasn't too much of a penance to work these hours. The financial reward also made it all worthwhile. It really was a great experience to see this giant construction project, by now nearing completion, taking shape day by day. That year seemed to fly by, and I had soon reached my designated twelve months' service at Sizewell.

It was on a sunny June day in 1965, when I was 19, that I finally learned of my next home move. I had never entirely taken to the county of Suffolk so, unlike previous moves, this one would hold no regrets.

At the power station there were two offshore maintenance platforms situated above the entrances to the intake and out-take seawater tunnels. The platforms were approximately 600 and 900 metres from the shoreline. From time to time it was the electricians' job to go and carry out maintenance on the platform cranes, and this involved rowing out and back in a small boat. These journeys had to be taken with great care and timing, as the shingle beach had no jetty.

Fortunately we always had an official boatman to accompany us on these tasks, otherwise something more serious than a severe dousing of seawater might have transpired. Returning from the crane platforms, you had to choose the right moment to leap off the boat, timing it in between waves and then scrambling quickly up the beach. The occasional wet foot was not unusual, but a mistimed manoeuvre could result in a soaking, to the considerable amusement of your workmates.

On this day we completed our work on the platform and had made a successful return to shore. Walking along the beach in front of me I could see a small group of people gathered around a ramshackle table. The electrical foreman, one of the site engineers and his assistant were sitting on some makeshift seats, sheltered by an improvised parasol. A few technical drawings were laid out across the table in random fashion. To me this all looked like some kind of a sham to get out of the office and enjoy some of the good seaside weather. They gestured for me to join them.

Once I got there, the foreman, Bill Weaver told me another site had been enquiring about my services and that the two other apprentices would also be on the move very shortly. Naturally I asked from where the enquiry had come from.

"Glamorgan" he said. He turned to his colleagues: "Where exactly is Glamorgan?" They looked at each other in silence. Clearly they were no wiser on that score than I was. In fact nobody seemed to have the faintest idea where I was going to be transferred to!

It was left for me to discover that Glamorgan was a county in South Wales and that the site was a mature open-cast coal mine at Pant-y-waun. This was an abandoned village high in the hills near a town called Merthyr Tydfil.

It was also left to me to find out that Merthyr Tydfil was some 270 miles away from Sizewell. In those days this was an enormous distance by United Kingdom standards. I was assured the company would pay all the cost of moving the caravan to South Wales, but because of its age I did not think having the caravan towed all that distance would do it any favours. I had to insist that transportation was conducted using a low-loader. The company readily agreed to this, and said there was a site available at Pant-y-waun. In addition there would be employment there for my mother, if she so wished.

One final thing needed to be confirmed in writing. When employees moved location, the company would pay a weekly subsistence allowance. In order to get this allowance a permanent home address had to be submitted. I could not record the caravan park as a permanent address and asked if could use my step-grandmother's home address in County Durham instead. After a meeting with David Morris, the site agent, this was agreed and I signed the agreement to transfer to another site. It was planned that I would locate there for approximately one year.

The move was under way, and it would be completed within the space of two weeks. Things were also moving just as fast with my fellow apprentices. Danny and Tony were being sent to sites at Middlesbrough in the north of England and Southampton in the south respectively.

We were all excited about our respective transfers. All of us had enjoyed our time at Sizewell and were confident that even better things lay ahead. Taylor Woodrow had a good reputation when it came to looking after their apprentices and promoting from within the company. If you were loyal to them, they in turn would feed your ambitions.

It was a still, bright late July morning in 1965 when the caravan park warden, Brian Wright, drove up with his tractor to hitch up our caravan and take it to be parked up at the caravan park entrance. A low loader was scheduled to arrive later that morning to take it on to South Wales. We had enjoyed a happy two and a half years there and were sorry to leave. The hard reality was that within the next two years, as the power station was completed and commissioned, a lot of other residents would also be moving away.

Our taxi arrived to take us to Saxmundham, where we would travel on the train to London on the first leg of our journey to South Wales. I thanked Brian Wright and pressed a £5 note into his hand. At first he didn't want to take the money, but I insisted. Without his help we might never have been able to buy the caravan and go to South Wales.

Getting into the taxi, we sped away from Leiston for the last time. We had arranged to spend the weekend at Lesley Watson's house. Afterwards we would travel on to begin a new chapter in our lives. A new homeland, a new job, new horizons beckoned. Surely nothing could go wrong now?

CHAPTER FIVE

A HOME IN THE
WELSH VALLEYS

After a pleasant weekend, we left the Watson family home early on Monday morning and travelled across London to Paddington station. It was time to board the train to South Wales. After some two and a half hours our journey entered the final stage and we arrived in the Welsh capital, Cardiff. Here we changed to a small diesel branch line train which creaked slowly out of the city en route to the town of Merthyr Tydfil.

After a few minutes I caught my first sight of the Taff Vale and the steep gorge around the village of Taff's Well. The sight of this landscape was awe-inspiring. It possessed rugged beauty the like of which I had never experienced before.

Suddenly, without warning, my mother began to cry. When I asked her what was wrong, she replied: "I didn't want to come to Wales!"

It was several minutes before she calmed down. I was completely taken aback at her reaction. Long before the day we left Leiston I had talked through the forthcoming move very thoroughly with her. There had been total agreement about every aspect of it. Perhaps I had not realised that she was fearful of going to an unknown part of the United Kingdom. But there was no turning back now.

The train continued up the valley, calling at different stations until we arrived at Merthyr Tydfil. We stepped out of the carriage. The day had been sunny and there was warmth in the air. I called a taxi and asked the driver to take us to the caravan park at Pant-y-waun, the address of the Taylor Woodrow open-cast coal mining site. The taxi driver seemed somewhat nonplussed as to where the caravan park was, but suggested that we go to Pant-y-waun and enquire there.

As we were driven through Merthyr High Street, I was impressed by the number and variety of shops, and I think my mother was too. She liked to go shopping and had had little opportunity to do so in many of our previous rural locations. I hoped the prospect of exploring this high street and others would make all the upheaval seem worthwhile after all.

I briefly cast my mind back to the scene some weeks previously on Sizewell beach. The people there that day did not seem to know where Glamorgan was. Maybe they didn't know, but by now, we certainly did!

The taxi journey took us on a steep climb up a seemingly endless hill. Eventually we emerged onto an upland plateau which can only be described as bleak and featureless. Our driver turned into a side road. The outlines of some large industrial buildings and parked earth moving vehicles came into view. We were at the opencast coal-mining site.

Suddenly I caught sight of our little caravan, and my heart sank. It was standing in the middle of an unmade courtyard opposite some scruffy corrugated iron buildings. After a 270-mile journey on a low-loader it had been set down right outside my new place of work. I just could not believe the situation that was confronting us and wondered what thoughts were going through my mother's mind.

I paid the taxi driver and he sped off back to Merthyr. Some workmen came over to speak to us and wanted to know who we were and why we had come there. Once I had explained, they invited us into the workshop and made us a very welcome cup of tea. It revived our flagging spirits.

I went over to the caravan and unlocked the door, wanting to see if anything had come adrift during the journey. To my great relief, everything was fine. A nearby house, used as a surveyor's office, was opened to provide washing facilities. We prepared to spend our first night in Wales in the most unforeseen circumstances.

The following morning could not come quickly enough for me. I was anxious to meet my new bosses and establish exactly how this dire situation had arisen. It was going to be a daunting task. At 19 one lacks the confidence or the negotiating skills of later life, and this was not a situation that I had foreseen or prepared for.

I didn't have long to wait. Soon I was in the presence of my immediate boss, electrical foreman Keith Norman, and the site agent, Mr Charles Carr. I shook hands with them and politely expressed my dismay at having our caravan parked in such a clearly unsuitable place. Their response was to tell me that their communications from the company at Sizewell had not included any information regarding my living requirements until the very last minute. A caravan park had never existed at Pant-y-waun in any shape or form. The village itself had long since been abandoned and now, as Taylor Woodrow extended their opencast mining operations, it awaited destruction.

At Sizewell there was a designated caravan park for the construction workers' senior staff. I had automatically assumed that a similar park existed at Pant-y-waun.

Politely but with conviction, I stressed that we could not possibly stay where we were. It was ludicrous to expect otherwise, especially as a pitching on a proper caravan park had been promised by the company.

This experience had taught me one thing: never totally trust any employer's word. Instead always look for flaws and loopholes in their presentation and promises. Not only had the company lied to me about the existence of a caravan park, they had lied about the job promised for my mother. There was no work for her in this place. In future I would have to be a little less trusting.

Another minor bombshell awaited me. Keith Norman and Charles Carr told me that the site working hours for engineering personnel were from 7 am to 7 pm Monday to Friday, ie a twelve-hour working day. On Saturday I would be expected to work from 7 am to noon. Sunday working was optional.

I knew that as the "new boy" on site, my opting to work less hours would not have given a very good impression. I felt I had to go along with this situation. There was consolation, in that a good income would be coming my way. Indeed this would be an opportunity to place some of my earnings into a savings account for the very first time. I could build for the future.

During the hours after our arrival at Pant-y-waun my mother showed great resilience. Far from being outwardly dismayed at the chaos, she carried on regardless. Her attitude was akin to the "spirit of the Blitz" exhibited by the residents of London during the war.

Keith Norman started a wide search of the district to look

for a suitable caravan park, but at the back of my mind was a contingency plan. If a suitable place could not be found, I would quit the company and have the caravan transported back to Leiston in the hope of finding some work with another company at Sizewell. The £50 in my savings account would be just enough to finance the return. I had no illusions that if I felt forced to do this, it would probably mean the end of my ambition to become an electrician.

Fortunately I never had to activate this "plan B". After three weeks of searching, Keith Norman came up with a solution. A vacancy had become available some 10 miles away at a caravan park in the village of Quaker's Yard, in a beautiful part of the Taff Valley. We would spend seven and a half very happy years at this place.

An employee was nominated to use a company Land Rover to tow the caravan done the valley to our new location. Bill Sage's tasks involved delivering and collecting heavy materials both on and off site. He conducted this work using a lorry which had a pick-up hydraulic arm permanently attached onto its loading platform.

Bill came from Tredegar, a town in a nearby valley, and was a very bubbly character. The Taylor Woodrow management held him in great esteem for his "can do" approach to tasks. This was all the more remarkable, as he had an artificial leg. A vehicle deemed the most suitable to tow our caravan away was selected.

Bill hitched up our caravan to the Land Rover and we all jumped in and drove over the plateau and down the valley to Quakers' Yard. It took a few twists and turns of the steering wheel before we could finally park the caravan on its nominated hardstanding pitch.

During the journey down my mother had constantly been

engaged in conversation with Bill. "It's really good that I can understand everything you say perfectly" she said.

"Well my dear, I've been around a bit you know" he replied.

My mother had been having some difficulty tuning in to the local dialect, but Bill, while having a lilt to his voice, spoke with an almost neutral accent.

I never did find out exactly how Bill had lost his leg. Despite this affliction he was a man who was always more than the equal of able-bodied people.

My mother and I settled in well at the caravan park. Any minor communication problems – the strong valley accents can initially be very confusing for someone more used to southern English ones – were soon dealt with. The extra money in my pay packet meant that my mother could go shopping without needing to be as frugal as before. Thanks to the very good public transport system we could afford trips to the seaside; Barry Island, Penarth and, by paddle steamer from Cardiff, Weston-super-Mare. We went inland to Brecon, travelling through beautiful mountain scenery. Then there was Pontypridd with its popular market days and Cardiff, a shopping paradise. At last life was good, and the future seemed bright.

By now I felt that I was on a real mission here in South Wales. I hoped that my mother would make some good new friends and that I would make progress, both on site and in college. Everyone had been very welcoming towards us, which more than made up for the awkward situation of the first three weeks. My new colleagues in the electrical department were a friendly collection of different characters.

The chargehand, Gustav Horvath, was the most prominent. Gus had come to South Wales after the suppression of the Hungarian uprising against Russian rule in 1956. He had determinedly overcome the many difficulties confronting a refugee at that time and slowly but surely he had established himself as a highly-respected employee.

Gus had great technical ability. This was frequently demonstrated when he was called upon to trace and fix complex electrical control systems using electrical fault-finding techniques. Unfortunately, when he tried to teach and instruct me in his ways, he lacked patience. As far as he was concerned I did not learn quickly enough, though if truth be told a good teacher will always help you overcome such slowness.

I learnt quickly never to lend Gus any items from my personal toolkit, as once used they would be quickly discarded and thrown in different directions! In spite of all this Gus was a good man, and I only wish I could have responded better to his demands.

Conditions on the open-cast mine site were a great contrast to the power station. In summer a dust cloud would often drift over the site and winter transformed it into a sea of mud. Nevertheless the camaraderie was excellent, probably due to the fact that, in order to endure these conditions, we all had to pull together or sink in the Pant-y-waun mud!

The company continued to sponsor my part-time education, and in September 1965 I went to enrol for a new course year at Merthyr College. When the attendance register was called on my first day of attendance, I had quite a shock. Some of the students had surnames like Nolan, O'Leary and Donovan. Even the lecturer was Mr McCarthy. They were clearly of Irish descent. This would not have been such a surprise to me had I known more about the history of South Wales, and Merthyr in particular. Eventually I found out that the town of Merthyr Tydfil and the neighbouring valley communities had all been part of a great industrial revolution. Some 150 years before, Merthyr had grown to become the largest and most powerful iron manufacturing centre, not just in the United Kingdom but in the world. This had attracted people from far and wide for what was to be the Welsh "Klondike" era.

As time went by some of the original immigrant families then sought out a new life and began emigrating to Pennsylvania in the north-eastern United States. Their work ethic and skill base would serve them well in the New World. There would be opportunities for the development of personal material wealth, and freedom to practise their respective religions. All this was the explanation for the diverse nature of the Merthyr students, whose great heritage has formed Wales into the modern, vibrant democracy it is today.

Slowly but surely, my mother and I settled into the everyday life of the area. The tears shed on the first day were soon a distant memory. We had come to love both our new environment and the people living in it. We had found somewhere to belong.

Now, for the first time in my working life, I was earning a real living wage, though only through working long hours. I was able to provide whatever my mother required for her housekeeping budget. With the excellent public transport system available we were able to make Sunday excursions to the seaside resort of Barry Island. Indeed life seemed good, and the future was bright.

Arthur and Lesley Watson, along with their youngest son Tony, came to South Wales on a visit to see us in our new surroundings. They found accommodation at a nearby bed-and-breakfast establishment.

We decided to spend a day at the seaside and travelled by train from Quakers Yard to Barry Island. While we were there we visited a tea shop on the Barry seafront for some light refreshment. For all the adversity in her life my mother put a brave face on for the world to see, and this especially applied when in the presence of her best friend.

"I wish I could be happy all the time, like you" the lady running the teashop remarked to my mother. "Well you have to try to be, don't you?" was the smiling reply. This was typical of someone who always tried hard to make the best of things, no matter what. We all went on to have a truly lovely afternoon.

In September 1966 my apprenticeship was completed and I became an electrician at last. With it came the awaited increase in pay and prestige. In my second year of college in Wales I had begun a new course at Llandaff Technical College in Cardiff. At college I had met other students on my course who were apprentices working in other industries and one fellow student, John Aherne, would tell me fascinating stories about his work in Cardiff's East Moors Steelworks. It seemed an interesting and dynamic place to work.

Life wasn't all work and study however, and my interest in football entered a new phase. I became a regular attender at both Cardiff City and Merthyr Tydfil Football Club matches. Watching these professional players perform, I felt the urge to play myself. On Sunday mornings I would walk to the neighbouring village of Edwardsville. There the local lads and I would play an improvised five-a-side football game on an old courtyard entrance.

Through this weekly get-together I got to know that Treharris Athletic FC, the local football club, were conducting twice-weekly training sessions which were being directed by a former professional player. Cyril Beech had played for Swansea Town and Birmingham City during his career. Now he was 40 and player-manager at Treharris Athletic. Cyril was a real fitness fanatic in every sense of the word. At first he had his work cut out trying to instil similar dedication into what was already a very good football team, but he had persisted and succeeded.

I went along one evening to watch the team train and it wasn't long before they invited me to join in. I found out very quickly that I could never hope to match the Treharris players' technique and skill levels. However when it came to fitness levels, I was up there with the best of them. I found myself attending Cyril's training sessions at every available opportunity, though my skills as a player were somewhat limited.

It was during one of these training sessions that I was made aware that my background was not that of the South Wales valleys, or indeed of Wales at all. During a momentary lull, the team's ace centre-forward, John Andrews, glanced at me inquisitively.

"You're English aren't you?" he said.

This form of identification had never really occurred to me, as most people living in England simply did not go around stating that they were English! My accent had triggered friendly curiosity among the players, hence the enquiry. It wasn't hostile in any way - on the contrary, I was made to feel very welcome. The training session continued without any further enquiries. John and his wife Barbara have remained my friends right up to the present day.

By now my mother had reached the age where she could receive the state pension, so there was no further need for her to worry about finding employment.

This was the time of my most formative years. With so many events and challenges happening, I never really had time to think about my mother's wartime letters, which were still stored inside one of the cupboards of our caravan. Indeed it never occurred to me that other workmates, friends and students had fully-structured family lives. In all this most of them had some kind of father figure, I didn't. Somehow I managed to lock away any thought of envy over this.

In my experience nothing in life moves in a straight line and, sure enough, change soon loomed on the horizon. Almost without warning, the company issued me with an instruction to transfer from the coal site to a power station in Pembroke, West Wales, within the next fortnight.

This instruction really should not have come as such a surprise to me. The original agreement had after all stipulated a one-year stay at Pant-y-waun, no longer, and I had now been there for almost two years. Taylor Woodrow classed people in this type of employment as "travelling men", who were always available for transfer at the drop of a hat. I was the only "travelling man" on the coal site.

However, something new had happened in the time since the agreement had been set up. For the first time in our lives, my mother and I had found somewhere to belong. It may have taken a little while, but now there was no denying it. We both now felt at home in Wales.

Had Taylor Woodrow instigated a move a year earlier, as planned, we might have accepted it. I thought Pembroke, although a very nice area, was too geographically isolated from the rest of the United Kingdom. It seemed like the end of the world.

During the days following the notice to move, I tried several stalling tactics in the faint hope that the company would withdraw its transfer instruction, but they were adamant that I had to leave Pant-y-waun.

One day the company's Chief UK Electrical Engineer came up from London on a site visit. Brian Carrington was a six-foot plus Australian who had a distinctive gold-capped front tooth and an air of authority to match. At Sizewell I had heard all about this man's notorious reputation for a firm, no-nonsense approach to electrical engineering problems and manpower planning.

He came into the electrical workshop, where I was working on the bench.

"Norman," he said, "I understand from Keith [Norman] that you are unwilling to move to Pembroke."

"Yes Mr Carrington, that's correct."

"I'm sorry to hear that. I have an electrician working on site there at the moment but he is on loan from Wylfa (Anglesey power station) and they want him back. I know you don't have a lot financially, and I feel this transfer would help you in that respect."

He paused for a few moments, seeing the reluctance written all over my face, and continued, "You see my predicament. I'll put it another way - I've had some good reports about you, and we don't want to lose you should you still refuse to go there."

This was a threat that wasn't even thinly veiled!

Over the days that followed the disagreement continued between myself and the company. It began to get acrimonious, and I had to act to stop matters deteriorating further. At my instigation, the first full-time union official ever to visit the site arrived to negotiate a satisfactory outcome for both parties.

The Electrical Trades Union Convenor, Mr Ivor Parton, rather took the Taylor Woodrow management by surprise. Suited and bespectacled, with a quiet but professional manner, he conducted the negotiations in a private meeting held in Mr Carr's office. I was not required to be in attendance, so I can only speculate that it was far removed from the anticipated shouting match popularly portrayed when union officials meet management.

Eventually an agreement was reached enabling me to leave the company on amicable terms, with the written offer of possible re-employment in the future. I felt that I had been loyal to the company, although my transfer there had been badly managed. In fact I had already sensed that my time at the coal site was up, and I had moved quickly behind the scenes to secure another job. John Aherne of Cardiff Steelworks had told me of the procedure for employment application there, and I now activated this in double-quick time. I received an invitation to attend an interview at the steelworks, and following the interview I was offered the post of maintenance electrician, which I gratefully accepted.

This new appointment was to be an exciting and challenging experience, with exposure to sophisticated control systems. I would be working with first-class engineers and a knowledgeable workforce.

After working in several areas of the steelworks I eventually established myself in the Melting Shop department. The Head of Electrical Engineering in that department was a man called Harry Meek, and he was one of the finest human beings I have ever had the privilege of working with. Harry had a proven track record of technical expertise and practical engineering, and he expected his workforce to apply their respective talents in the same way. He always insisted that the safety of his staff was paramount, and practised due diligence to ensure that this was upheld. I enjoyed working under his direction. After a year had passed by he promoted me to the post of acting day electrical chargehand. This would be made permanent, pending higher management approval.

There was a story doing the rounds in the steelworks relating to Harry's wartime service in the Royal Air Force. It was said that he had once had occasion to rescue a pilot from an aircraft that had burst into flames. I do not know if this was an authentic account of events, but I can say this with absolute certainty - if Harry had ever been faced with such a situation then he would, without question, have acted accordingly.

Meanwhile, back at home in Quakers' Yard, I had been unaware that my mother had been having spells of ill-health with incidents of dizziness and headaches but bravely carrying on as normal. We had been able to take holidays at the seaside and visit the cinema and theatres. I took her back to north-east England to see her stepmother, Ethel Spencer, because I knew she was always pleased to return to the north-east and in particular to Barnard Castle.

Now I had another target in mind - to buy our own house. Before that, I needed something more practical than my second-hand motor scooter to take me around. After passing my driving test the second time around, I bought my first covered vehicle, a three-wheeled Reliant Robin. This proved to be great fun to drive, though you had to take great care when braking and cornering as Robins had a reputation of taking off and turning over!   The outer bodywork was constructed of glass fibre, and this led to some of my workmates giving my car the nickname "the flying eggshell".

In 1971 I started to search in earnest for a house. It would have to be in or near to Cardiff to ease my daily journey to the steelworks. The driving force was the burning desire to put an end to our previous nomadic lifestyle once and for all. There was also the desire for a feeling of security which comes when you own your own property. I also wanted my mother to be able to live in greater comfort, and to be able to invite friends into our home with no feeling of inferiority.

One Friday in October I happened to be in Caerphilly

when I chanced upon an advertisement in an estate agent's window. It read: "Two Bedroom Semi-Detached Bungalows for sale in a forthcoming new development at Tir Merchant Farm Caerphilly. A deposit of £50 is required".

My mother had been having increasing problems walking and had always opposed the idea of buying a house, because that would mean climbing stairs. These bungalows seemed to be an ideal solution. I made an immediate enquiry at the estate agent's office and they gave me directions to the building site.

When I got there I found myself surveying a field in which the installation of drainage sewers and foundations was in the early stages. But I had seen enough, and returned to the estate agent. I had only £30 with me that day and had to return on the following Monday with the outstanding £20.

That winter seemed to drag on for an eternity. I would visit the building site every so often to check on progress and ask the latest estimate for the completion date, and began to think about buying furniture for our new home. Eventually I was informed that April 22nd 1972 was to be the big day when our first permanent home would officially become ours, though it would be twenty years before the mortgage was finally paid off.

Leaving the Quakers Yard Caravan Park for the last time was a bit of a wrench. The week before our departure I sold the caravan, our home for 10 years, for a nominal sum. It had served us well.

The day when I would be officially handed the keys to the house arrived at last. I went to the housing estate to complete the fitting of some curtain rails and was handed the keys by the builder's representative.

For me, and I hoped for my mother, it was a momentous milestone. On that great day I recalled all the other places where we had lived. Always they were houses belonging to someone else, where we were in effect just passing through. In all they totalled twenty-four different locations, all but the last three of which involved sharing someone else's home. After leaving the convalescent home in London NW1, they were as follows:

January 1946: Knightsbridge, London
September 1946: Eridge, Kent
August 1948: Yarmouth, Isle of Wight
March 1949: Canterbury, Kent
March 1950: New Romney, Kent
December 1952: Wickham Market, Suffolk
February 1953: West Hendred, Berkshire
January 1954: Brampton, Huntingdonshire
March 1954: Kingswood, Surrey
November 1954: Loxwood, Sussex
March 1955: Greatham, Hampshire
January 1957: Cobham, Surrey
July 1957: Hertford, Hertfordshire
August 1957: Roydon, Essex
February 1959: Coggeshall, Essex
January 1961: Lexden, Colchester, Essex
February 1961: Little Horkesley, Colchester, Essex
April 1961: Thorrington Cross, Brightlingsea, Essex
June 1961: Coggeshall, Essex
September 1961: Benhall, Suffolk
April 1962: Aldringham, Suffolk
September 1962: St George's Caravan Park, Leiston, Suffolk.
August 1965: Pant-y-Waun, Glamorgan
September 1965: Quaker's Yard Caravan Park, Glamorgan

Now at last, in the spring of 1972, a new, more settled and secure way of life was beginning.

The seven years following our arrival in South Wales had been busy and eventful, and I had not given a second thought as to who or where my father was, or even if I needed him. We soon settled into our new bungalow and consequently my journey to work was now shorter, the shops nearer and the living space more spacious.

Alas, we could not bring our neighbours with us, and for the first few months my mother missed them greatly. To help compensate a little for this, Lesley and Arthur Watson came down from London to stay for a few days. They were impressed by our new home. Arthur had confided in me that he feared his wife would now want the same type of property. He wondered how this could be done, as house prices were vastly more expensive in and around London.

When August came around, we took a little holiday at Bournemouth on the south coast of England and returned refreshed. But the happiness was not to last. A few weeks after our return, my mother suffered the first of a series of strokes which were to see her hospitalised for lengthy periods. As a result she was never able to be fully able to enjoy her new home and surroundings, though she always made valiant efforts to do so.

A good neighbour, Eiddwen Hudson, offered to help with some of the housework in return for a small fee. I readily accepted this kind offer, which also meant that my mother would have someone nice to talk to during the day.

After a couple of years Eiddwen's increased family commitments meant that this was no longer possible, so I placed an advertisement for help in the window of one of the local shops. Joyce Edwards, from the neighbouring village of Bedwas responded to my request. Originally from London, she had married South Walian Verner Edwards after a wartime romance during the Blitz. Joyce was an honest, hard-working lady who not only cleaned my house but provided my mother with pleasant company.

I continued to study one day a week at technical college. During free periods we often went to the library to focus on our respective core subjects, and sometimes I found myself also reading books on subjects that had nothing whatsoever to do with my trade. Publications on WWII particularly fascinated me.

After a few weeks one of my fellow students commented, "Norm, you should have been an electrician in the war". At the time it was just another amusing remark, but in later years it would have a certain irony about it.

At the steelworks, other problems were looming. For many years it had become apparent that new investment in plant and machinery was needed. The steelmaking furnaces were well past their sell-by date. A change of government had resulted in the cancellation of a promised release of funds.

Then it was announced that the works was to close in 3–5 years' time. From a personal point of view, it was again time for action. After several interviews with different companies, I secured the post of Maintenance Electrician at the Wiggins Teape Papermill in the west of Cardiff.

For my first few weeks at the paper mill it was a case of *déjà vu*, with a swift settling-in period among my new colleagues. Once again they were almost without exception very friendly, and the workplace had something akin to a family atmosphere about it. In later years this would change perceptibly. Increased consumerism would lead to more competiveness among the workforce, while management, under great pressure to meet rising targets, would impose higher demands for productivity and efficiency.

February 17th 1976 started out cold and frosty. I visited my mother in hospital early in the morning. As she had now lost the power of speech, communication was difficult for her. Later on that day I went to a local technical college, where I had enrolled on a fast-track electronics course in order to keep up with some of the new developments. I was really glad to get home that evening, as it had snowed a little earlier that day and the bad weather was closing in.

At 9. 30 pm, the doorbell rang. I opened the door. My policeman neighbour Steve was standing outside. This was clearly no social call, as he was in his uniform. I instinctively knew what he was about to tell me.

"Norm, I've called about your mother," he said. "Norm – I'm very sorry, she's passed away. "

My mother had died earlier that evening. It had happened very quickly, without warning and without any visible pain or distress. A new milestone had occurred in my life – an unwanted one, though one which most of us have to endure at some stage or other in our lives.

CHAPTER SIX

A SHOCKING DISCOVERY

Now I had the task of telephoning Lesley Watson in London to inform her of the sad news. Back then the nearest telephone was a call box several hundred yards from my home. My footsteps were heavy as I walked, and I felt the cold February air biting my skin more than usual.

After a few minutes I reached the call box, placed the appropriate coins in the slot and began to dial. For some reason, maybe it was the tension of the moment, I misdialled. When someone answered the phone I immediately said, "Norman speaking. I have some very bad news".

A voice came back down the line, "This is Norman! What do you want?" I do not know the odds of mistakenly dialling someone with the same first name, but nevertheless it had happened.

Eventually, after redialling, I managed to get through to convey the news to Lesley. She expressed her condolences and promised to travel down with her husband Arthur to attend the funeral. Next there was the task of calling Doris' step-mother Ethel in Retford, Nottinghamshire (she had moved there in 1975 together with Mrs Rose Dixon and her daughter Brenda).

I finished by calling two of my former steelworks colleagues, Richard Jones and Harry Meek. They had both been most sympathetic about my home situation, which had not been a total surprise, for they were very respected colleagues of mine.

No matter how expected a person's death may be, when it finally happens there is an air of unreality about it all. My mind went back to one of the few occasions when I had had to lie to my mother. After the first stroke she had often had dizzy spells, but she usually recovered after a few minutes. Many times she had posed the question "will I get better?" and many times I had said, "of course you will – it may take a little while but you will". Now I had to begin the inevitable procedure when someone dies – obtaining a death certificate and contacting an undertaker. Having no relatives to assist me, my mind was entirely focused on the task in hand, and in a way this helped to suppress my grief.

The day of the funeral arrived exactly a week after my mother's passing and, as is often the case in these events, much of it was a complete blur to me. However three particular moments have stayed with me from that day, and always will.

The route of the cortège took us through the centre of Caerphilly and along the mountain road over to the crematorium at Thornhill, Cardiff. Slowly we wended our way through the town, where we encountered a red traffic light at a junction. Instinctively, without a second thought, an elderly gentleman standing on the street corner removed his cap and stood bolt upright with his head bowed as a mark of respect. I wanted to jump out of the funeral car and shake his hand, but realistically this was not possible.

Steadily we made the steep journey up the Caerphilly mountain road, always in sight of the hearse. The pale February sun was now shining through and Arthur Watson made a poignant remark: "How nice for the sun to be out on the day of Doris' final journey".

After what seemed an eternity, the cortège finally arrived at the crematorium reception area. From the window of the funeral car I saw, among the waiting mourners, three familiar figures. Douglas Cook, Billy Hughes and Gerry Davies, my colleagues from the Paper Mill, were standing together on the grass verge. I was deeply moved by their consideration in attending my mother's funeral. They had never met her.

With the funeral and the initial aftermath over, it became my task to transport the casket containing my mother's ashes "back home" to Barnard Castle. I had made arrangements for interment in the grave of the grandparents who had effectively undertaken her upbringing following the death of her mother, Susan.

Some weeks later I made the 300-mile journey north by car, taking the precious casket with me. The day of the interment in "Barney" was one of intermittent showers as I drove the short distance from my step-grandmother's home to the churchyard. There were just three people at the graveside as the casket was gently placed in the excavated plot. At that very moment a shaft of sunlight shone through the clouds, and I had the feeling that my mother had finally returned home after a lifetime away. It seemed like confirmation that I had made the right decision all round.

During the weeks that followed, I had good days and bad days, as we all experience following a bereavement. Neighbours, friends, workmates and team-mates all helped with sympathetic words and deeds.

My new situation was eased somewhat by weekly invitations to the homes of Colin Phipps and David Jackson. Colin was a former colleague of mine at the steelworks, a flamboyant but softly-spoken man with a large house and family. Somehow he had got word of events and appeared unexpectedly, with his wife Jenny, at the funeral.

David Jackson was also a softly-spoken person, but his background could not have been more different. An Oxford-educated university lecturer, he had got to know me through playing and training with Rhiwbina football club in Cardiff. David had written to me expressing his sympathy and inviting me to his home, where I was to meet Alison, his wife.

The time eventually came when I had to begin the difficult but inevitable task of the disposal of the majority of my mother's personal possessions, with the exception of those items which held sentimental value. Every person has to go through this procedure when someone close to them passes away. I was given the good advice not to let this course of action linger but to activate it quickly, so as not to extend the grieving process. Eventually this was completed, but not before a discovery was made which was to change my outlook on life for many years ahead.

I opened a drawer in her dressing table and there it was, the little bundle of letters I'd come across years before when we'd been living in our little caravan in Leiston. I remembered that at that time one particular letter had caught my eye, or to be more precise a few lines in it, written in an affectionate tone and followed by the signature "Joe". I'd asked who Joe was, to which my mother had replied that he was an American she had known during the war. And that what was that. Since that time I had had no idea where she had put them and had thought no more about that brief interlude. But now I had this bundle of letters in my hand, and had time to examine them more thoroughly.

The bundle contained a lot of correspondence from Marion Prideaux, along with some from other former employers and friends. As I went along I tried to separate out those that seemed to have come from the mysterious Joe. It wasn't easy, since there were several loose, numbered pages but only one with a letterhead. Some of the pages were incomplete. I looked at an intact section numbered 11, which read thus:

The leaves and furloughs may come soon and especially those in the flying crews. I don't know when that will be but we've been assured that all possible facilities will be tried in order to get those to England that wish to go there. Was in Paris close to a fortnight ago for a few hours and the food situation is very critical, even worse than England. An American or British soldier can't be served in a civilian restaurant. Thank God there were several American Red Cross clubs and NAAFI clubs where you could get a bit of lunch.

Another loose, fragmented page, numbered 111, read:

…and ring you up, but you can rest assured that your every wish will come true within reason when that memorable occasion of a furlough in England comes. This time we will really do it up and when the time is up we will both have had enough for several fortnights at least. I think of you often, as several pleasant memories seem to filter into the horrible image of war with its course but real and unbelieving marks which never can heal.

I unfolded another fading, typed sheet of paper which seemed to originate from another wartime letter. This one read:

War is a hard thing to face and all English people are aware of that fact. Met a lot of Tommies in a neighbouring village who are sweating out "blighty leave" and we talked a great deal about England. In all the fellows I talked to I didn't meet any from up Barnard Castle way and any who knew a Peter Spencer.

If the situation arises that I should never see you again, such as going home or to a different theatre of operations, I still want to hear from you regularly. If the war should end soon (and God grant that it does) I'm planning a visit to England, whether it be in uniform or in civvy street. I don't want to bore you with the life of a soldier, so I'll tell you that the next time we get to Paris or any other big city of any size I'll get you something that all girls like, namely perfume. When the hair pins come I'll send them.

Write soon and in the meantime I'm getting sufficient rest and hoping that I get leave soon. I'm not fooling around with the French much and a glass of wine has been my greatest indulgence. Therefore I should give a showing for myself. Again I say, write soon and let me know if all is well and if there is still that feeling remaining between us.

All my love,
Joe.

By now I had become enthralled by the discovery of this bundle of letters, although it felt as if I was prying into my mother's past private life. Sifting through the collection, I began to separate items from Joe and other communications. I then came across what appeared to be a complete letter, together with an envelope bearing a United States franked postmark. It was addressed thus;

Miss Doris Spencer
Hamsell Lake
Eridge
Sussex, England

The top left-hand corner of the envelope bore the name and address of the sender (as is the custom in the US). The writing had deteriorated with age, with the result that the sender's name was almost illegible. As far as I could make out, it read:

J. Schwart(z) (or y)
West Lodge, Ypsilanti
Michigan
USA

The letter itself was in better condition, and I started to read it.

West Lodge, Ypsilanti
Michigan
October 19th 1946

Dear Doris,

I have been turning over quite a bit of news in my head and have finally assimilated it enough in my head to make a bit of sense. At the close of the summer term I took a short vacation and have recently returned. Needless to say your news was very revealing and very surprising. After reading your letter, I was stunned and it took me several days to regain my composure. It doesn't make sense and when your second letter arrived, it renewed my perplexity. I'm really at a loss as far as doing anything is concerned.

This institution is rated third in the U. S. for what I am studying and it taxes my energies. Living on my very <u>limited</u> income is hard, especially when prices for everything are at this level. There is one ray of hope however, and it occurred several days ago. I've made enquiries and I've reasonable knowledge that I can secure a radio operators licence from the government. Then next summer, it will greatly cut down on expenses *if I'm able to work my passage over and back in that capacity.*

When I am at my studies everything else is immaterial. In other words I lose contact with everything around me. It's like living a "cloistered life". It must be like this in order to make sufficiently high grades, if you don't, out you go.

Many have been given the "boot" already. If, in the future, my letters are few and far apart, that will be the most influential factor in it being like that.

In closing, let me say that this is all very confusing to me. It's hard to believe because of the peculiar situation. As far as marriage is concerned, I'm still single and aim to remain so for a few years yet - that is until my studies are completed. We hardly knew each other and I believe there is quite an age gap between us. My age is 25.

Well Doris, don't fret because I'm not capable of doing anything at this time or I can't say when I'll be. If possible I'll try and make it this coming summer. Continue writing and I'll try and answer promptly. Incidentally, how about a picture of you and while we're speaking of you, what plans have you made concerning us?

Joe.

P.S. I may not be at this institution long as I've been given a good offer at another one. If I've left by the time your letter arrives, they'll forward it to me. What price SUCCESS.

It did not take me more than a few seconds to realise that this letter was about a romantic affair between my mother and the mysterious Joe. Now I began to search among the bundle for further information. The vast majority of the remaining letters appeared to originate from Marion Prideaux, with her distinctive handwriting and affectionate, caring messages of support. I quickly placed these aside one by one, until I came across a typewritten page written on airmail paper. The top half of the page had become detached and was missing, but the remaining contents riveted my attention. It was not the wafer-thin paper that first attracted me but rather the fountain pen signature at the bottom of the page. It bore the by now familiar name "Joe".

I read the contents above the signature, then I read it again and again until I could read it no more. Many emotions passed through my mind in those few brief minutes, but the overriding one was this: I had found the real reason for my dear mother's reluctance to discuss Joe. He was my missing biological father.

It now appeared that my father had not after all perished in the war but had survived it, and had begun to study at an institution in America.

The typed air mail half-sheet read thus:

During my stay at school I met a schoolmate whose father had interests in South America as well as the States. On several occasions his sister came to Ann Arbor to visit him. We became very attached to one another and this led to intimate relations on several occasions at one of the local hotels where she was staying.

Six weeks ago she came to Ann Arbor to visit him. It was then that I discovered she was pregnant, and she proved conclusively that I was the father of her expected child.

Now I am in St Louis, living with her parents and learning her father's business. As soon as I learn the business I shall leave for South America to work in the branch office there. After the child is born, Mary will follow as soon as possible.

Mary my wife knows all about our relationship and has the utmost sympathy for you, but under the existing circumstances it was either she or you, and she is here.

My intentions concerning you were always sincere, but fate is very unpredictable at times.

I trust that you will appreciate the true gravity of the situation. As for Norman, I believe that you'll have the intelligence to tell him some story of his father's death during the war, or another story equally acceptable, when he is old enough to understand.

Take care of yourself, and I hope that this episode of your life will come to an end when you finally marry some Englishman of your choosing.

With everlasting love,
Joe.

I felt an inner feeling of anger as I read this. In effect my father was writing me off as a person in a few well-crafted lines. I vowed that no one in future would ever be given the opportunity to do this.

After, for want of a better phrase, catching my breath, I went about finalising the scrutiny of the remaining letters and making sure there was nothing else from "Joe" that I had missed. Indeed I had not missed anything, until I then made another discovery. There in among the aforementioned items was a sepia photograph of what appeared to be a full-faced military officer. Turning the picture over, I found the following handwritten inscription:

Joseph Schwartz [or possibly Schuranty – I couldn't be sure]
703 Church St
Ann Arbor
Michigan
U.S.A.

Putting two and two together very quickly, it seemed that the photograph was that of the mysterious Joe, who had now been brought out of the shadows to become Joseph Schwartz (Schuranty) - my father, residing at an address in the United States.

A myriad thoughts now began to run through my mind. The overriding one was - where is Joseph Schwartz (Schuranty) today? One thing was certain. There were some questions I wanted to ask him, and I hoped for some honest answers.

CHAPTER SEVEN

THE HUNT BEGINS

I now gave the wartime photograph special scrutiny. The inscription on the back posed a question. The surname was not written in a way that made it easy to identify, and could have been Schwartz or Schuranty. However, putting two and two together very quickly it seemed that the photograph was that of the mysterious Joe, who had now been brought out of the shadows to become my father, and that he was residing in a town called Ann Arbor, Michigan State, USA.

I wondered where exactly in Michigan this place called Ann Arbor was, and what type of people lived there. A visit to the local library in Caerphilly enabled me to define its location. I thought about writing to the Church Street address to enquire as to the current whereabouts of Joseph Schwartz. Also passing through my mind was the significant content of the air mail letter, which leaned towards the distinct possibility that my father was by now living in South America.

The rest of 1976 seemed to fly by as I adjusted to my new circumstances. I began to enjoy playing football again and reconstructing my social life. My only practical attempt to trace my father had been in the form of a letter written to the occupier of 703 Church Street, Ann Arbor, asking for any information on the whereabouts of Joseph Schwartz/Schuranty. Needless to say, no reply was forthcoming. This non-response had done nothing to quell the thought that my father had indeed gone to South America with his new wife and baby and was indeed at this time enjoying "SUCCESS". South America is of course a vast continent, and if ever there was a case of finding a "needle in a haystack", this was it.

I showed my friend David Jackson the inscription on the back of the sepia photograph and sought his opinion on the interpretation of the surname. David thought it was Schwartz, but I have to say that I was still not sure.

On my next visit to see my step-grandmother, Ethel Spencer, and her friend Rose Dixon in Retford I posed the same question: "Was my father's surname Schwartz, or Schuranty, or something similar?" I was given the reply that it had been Schwartz. For some reason I still had doubts about the authenticity of the name, but I put it to one side for the time being.

The spring of 1977 was a particularly good one weather-wise, and as an added bonus the management at the paper mill nominated me, along with two other colleagues, to attend a three-day electronic drive control training course in Kingsbury, North London. We travelled to London looking forward to a change from our everyday working routines in the mill.

It had been agreed between us beforehand that on completion of the course we could travel home independently on different trains, if so desired. I was particularly keen to do this, as I intended to take the opportunity to make a visit to the United States Embassy in Grosvenor Square. My hope was that in presenting my father's photograph showing him in military uniform, with a probable home address inscribed on the back, more information would be forthcoming. I would soon find out how naive this assumption was.

In those days you could enter the embassy unchallenged. I walked up to the reception desk and gave a brief outline of my request and the reason for it. I was given instructions to stand on one side by a nominated telephone and wait for it to ring. After what seemed an eternity the phone rang, and I found myself listening to someone with as a very strong accent originating from the deep south of the US.

After I had given my story, the reply came back down the line: "What makes you think we would have any information about this man here? There were thousands of US soldiers in Europe during World War Two. We are very busy, so please go away and do not waste our time any more, thank you, goodbye."

I felt completely numbed and hurt by this insensitive response, and could not get out of the building quick enough. This demoralising experience was not what I had expected or been prepared for. It had the effect of shutting out all thoughts of tracing Joseph Schwartz/Schuranty for some time, though the dilemma remained in my subconscious mind.

On my return home after this setback I found another disappointment was in store for me, which put such things into a different perspective. Joyce Edwards had continued to come along to my house twice a week to do a little cleaning, but she had been suffering with the early onset of lung cancer. Her condition had meant she was no longer able to assist me. In no time at all I found myself visiting her in hospital, where, after some pain, she passed away. 1977 had been a year to forget.

In late spring, a peony plant always produces beautiful blooms in my garden. It was given to me by Joyce, and the scent from it always serves to remind me what a kind, loving person she was. Some people have an inner beauty which is not always obvious to the casual observer.

In 1979 there was much speculation in the media as to how much lower the price of transatlantic flights would fall. A new era of low-cost air travel instigated by the Australian entrepreneur Freddie Laker had been making headlines. Somehow Laker had managed to break the cartel operated by the major airline companies, and as a result travel to America became available to the general public. I had always wanted to see America and that November, armed with the knowledge that I was almost certainly half American, I began to look for inexpensive flights and accommodation.

One particular travel company, Trek America, caught my attention. It offered a combination of low-cost flights and camping expeditions led by a US national leader-driver. From the list of expeditions I selected the three-week coast-to coast "Southerner" and made my booking.

The Southerner had caught my attention because the tour itinerary took you through New York and Washington and hence through several of the states that had declared their allegiance to the Confederacy during the civil war of 1861-65. The Confederacy at this time in history had always intrigued me, and I felt some connection with them as underdogs in the conflict. In particular I have always felt great admiration for their military leader, General Robert E. Lee. Lee had made a proclamation around this time: "It is good that war is so terrible, lest we should grow fond of it". This has always lodged in my mind as a very true and thoughtful observation of one of mankind's greatest weaknesses, the desire to dominate other nations and people.

With the booking made for the trip and my application for a visa duly approved, it was only a matter of a few weeks before my transatlantic journey in August. One month before my trip I paid a fleeting visit to the home of Arthur and Lesley Watson at the south coast resort of Bognor Regis, where they had moved to enjoy retirement by the seaside.

I remembered a story they had told me about something that happened when I visited them as a little boy. Apparently the radio began to play some American military music. Without prompting I had marched back and forth across the room, saluting. The Watsons and my mother had looked at each other in astonishment. The comment at the time was along the lines, "We don't know how, but somehow he knows about his American father".

Now Lesley and Arthur were both intrigued about my forthcoming trip to America. Lesley went further, and gently asked me if, during my time over there, I would be looking for my father. I said that the trek route did not go anywhere near to Michigan State, so it would only be possible to gain a general impression of my father's country and nothing more.

Sensing my obvious discomfort at her question, Lesley added: "Try not to feel unhappy about your father. He did what he thought was best at the time". She then stated that since my birth, "Joe was the only man in your mother's life". This was a well-meant observation, but it did nothing to quell the anger and frustration I felt.

Sadly, a few weeks later Lesley passed away, and another link with my mother had gone forever.

On a fine morning in early August 1980, I boarded the Freddie Laker Skytrain at London Gatwick en route to New York, where I would meet up with 11 other travellers from

Europe. Although I was now 34, this was my first flight. I was surprised how steeply the plane climbed after take-off. There was no fear about this, more of a fascination that something so big and heavy could be controlled and manoeuvred with such ease.

The eight hours airborne seemed to pass by quickly, and soon we were touching down at Kennedy Airport. It was now dusk, and the first impression was how poor the artificial lighting was. Was this really the land of my father? Was this the country which in my early years, had inspired the music to which I had marched up and down the room whenever it was played on the radio? Was this the glamorous place I had seen on the Hollywood movies, indeed the one that was supposed to be in my blood? It seemed to be yet another instance of the difference between imagination and reality.

As if to underline this, the arrival at my pre-booked hotel in Manhattan was equally uninspiring. The trek company had given instructions for me to take a service bus link from Kennedy Airport to the East Side terminal in Manhattan. From there I had been directed to take a cab to the hotel, but under no circumstances should I share it with anyone I did not know. I had elected to do just this with someone I had struck up a conversation with while waiting in line at the immigration desk. I had spotted a "Trekamerica" label on the luggage of another passenger. Young female trekker Virginia Brown was apparently bound for the same intended destination as myself. She was going on a different trek from mine, but would be staying at the same hotel overnight. We agreed to share a cab.

After a seemingly endless bus journey along gloomy highways, we eventually arrived in Manhattan. Here various bus drivers were busy emptying the holds of luggage. There seemed to be a competition going on to see who could throw the various items furthest along the pavement! We were not excluded from this contest, but we managed to retrieve our individual baggage without it succumbing to serious damage.

I hailed a cab and we asked to be taken to the Prince George Hotel. Suddenly a young man, who had obviously heard my request, opened the cab door and asked to share the journey with us. Although his British West Country accent was reassuring, I remembered my prior instructions and refused his request. The door closed and we sped off.

Arriving at the Prince George was an impressive experience. This vast, looming building looked like something out of King Kong. The interior was no different - vast oak panels were in proliferation, and the man at the reception desk had the appearance and manner of a Hollywood extra. If James Cagney ever had a modern-day double then this was him, but maybe the theory that you grow to look like your surroundings explained this.

Virginia and I checked in, then entered the creaking oak-panelled elevator and ascended to the floors of our respective rooms. The trek company had pre-booked mine on a sharing basis to keep costs down. At the time of my departure from the UK I had not been made aware of who my room-mate would be, but this was a minor detail. It was all part of the adventure.

I found the room number and unlocked the door. It was unoccupied, so I decided to take a brief soak in the bath and settle down to watch television. It must have been around half an hour later when the key began to turn in the lock. My fellow room-mate for the night emerged. It was the young man I had refused to share the cab with!

"Ah, we meet again," he said. "My name's Dave."

I had started my first night in America with an embarrassing moment. It was time for some apologies and some sleep.

The following morning everyone met up in the hotel foyer and we were introduced to our travelling companions for the next three weeks and the leader/driver of the trek. Our route would take us from New York to Washington DC, through Virginia, Tennessee, Alabama and down to New Orleans. From there we would travel across Texas, calling in at Galveston, San Antonio and El Paso. Next came Tombstone before heading further up through Arizona to the Grand Canyon. The final leg would be across the desert to Las Vegas before arriving at our final destination, Los Angeles.

I received many impressions of America, its people, history and infrastructure. During the three weeks I was spending there I had hoped to experience some kind of connection with the country. This did not happen, and I came away a little disillusioned about it all.

In 1982 a newspaper article about an organisation called the "Friendship Force" appeared in the South Wales press. The organisation had been founded by President Jimmy Carter and was based in Atlanta, Georgia. Its purpose was to organise voluntary exchanges between groups of people in America and the rest of the world. I discovered that a local branch had been formed in Cardiff. I attended several of the meetings and registered to go on an exchange visit to the town of Lancaster, Pennsylvania. My hope was that I would get to know grassroots America by living with an American family for a fortnight. This would, I hoped, give me an insight of what life might have been like had my father returned post-war and taken me back home.

In early August I arrived at Cardiff Airport, where several groups of people had assembled to wait for the arrival of our charter aircraft. There was great excitement when the navigation lights of our Transamerica jet suddenly appeared out of the sky. Cardiff being a small airport, we were ready to board in no time at all. A group of Pennsylvanians had disembarked, for they were going to stay in the homes of Cardiff Friendship Force members.

Soon the plane was taxiing down the runway ready for take-off. On board was a young teenage girl who would be disembarking at our next stop, Newcastle, England. Her name was Amy Carter - she was the former President's daughter. A visit to Washington in County Durham had been planned for her, where she would see the place where some of her ancestors came from. She was accompanied by an entourage of security personnel.

We made a very heavy landing at Newcastle - not for the faint hearted or the first-time flyer. Another exchange of Friendship Force passengers took place and then we took off again, bound for Shannon Airport in the Irish Republic. This was the final exchange before Pennsylvania. The Shannon landing was also bumpy and our final touchdown at Harrisburg Airport was due for the late evening. There was a certain amount of apprehension about our scheduled night-time landing. This time however, it was a perfect touchdown, followed by a round of applause!

On leaving the aircraft, we found ourselves staring into a bank of spotlights. The local media were filming our arrival and announcing it to all and sundry. It wasn't Hollywood, but if felt a little like it.

Introductions to our respective hosts followed. I had already written to the host family, the Thompsons, some weeks earlier and knew a little about them. I had been paired with Brian

Trerise, a Cardiffian. We were to share a room together and we would do our best to learn about America and the host family. In turn we would give information about our own homeland.

The Thompsons were more than welcoming to us, and it was really nice to be accepted by them. We enjoyed trips to Washington, Philadelphia, Gettysburg and the local attractions. On the longer trips I did the driving, as Brian had somehow managed to leave his driving licence at home.

There were also social events and shopping trips. During one of these something happened which remains in my mind to the present day. We had been to one of the local supermarkets and one of the store assistants had begun to load our purchases into the boot of Charol's car. He said, "I'd like to help you more ma'am, but I guess you've got an all-American boy with you to assist". He was looking straight at me. For the very first time, albeit unwittingly, I had been identified as an American in my father's homeland.

When there was some free time, I would often play a game of improvised tennis against Chad Thompson. He was only five years old but would always score the winning points of the game. It was important to ensure that his confidence was kept high! After noticing this Charol remarked that I would be a good father to someone. It was flattering to hear this sentiment.

I think both Brian and I were very appreciative of the generosity of spirit afforded towards us by our host family and enjoyed our experience of life in America at grass roots level. I came away from this trip with a little more knowledge of everyday life there but, in reality, no further clues as to the whereabouts of my father. Always at the back of my mind there lay the desire and hope that one day I would meet him and his family. It would be a sunny day, perhaps in a typical mid-west town. We would compare notes about our respective lives and talk about my mother and his reasons for abandoning his proposed post-war return to England.

On my return to Wales, the workplace was becoming ever more challenging, thanks to the pace of technological change. This was not proving to be an easy transition. At least there was a chance to escape from this in the form of my sporting activities. But time was catching up with me and I was becoming more and more injury prone. At the end of the 1983-84 season, approaching 40, I decided to call it a day. Over a period of 17 years I had played parks football for nine different teams in the Cardiff and District leagues. Time, like the tide, does not wait for anyone. My days of playing in competitive matches were over.

In the spring of 1984 I happened to read a holiday feature in one of the Sunday newspapers referring to the "best beaches in the Mediterranean". Now that the desire to see America had retreated somewhat, I decided that a change of holiday venue would be desirable. One of the places listed in the article was the French island of Corsica.

I made a booking for a week's package holiday in the seaside resort of Algajola. On arrival in late June at this beautiful, laid-back location, I felt that my choice had been a good one.

It must have been on my second day in Algajola that I somehow got into conversation with one of the German holidaymakers there. This was no surprise, as there was a large contingent from Germany staying in the village. My stereotypical image of Germany and the Germans had always been a rather dour one, tainted by the incorrect assumption in my early life that they had been responsible for my father's demise. A few minutes' conversation on the beach rapidly dispelled this inbuilt prejudice.

Dieter Pfab, his girlfriend Brigitte, her brother Hansie and their friend Michael Grillmair enlightened me about their life back home. They came from Bavaria. For the rest of the week we spent a lot of time together on the beach and in Algajola village. When the time came to go our separate ways, they extended an invitation for me to visit them in Bavaria the following year.

In September 1985, after I had re-established contact with my beach friends, I took a £99 Pan-Am flight from London to Munich for a week's visit. There to meet me at Munich airport were several of the people I had met on Algajola beach. They had taken the time and trouble to welcome me to their homeland. For the next seven days I had an unforgettable introduction to every aspect of Bavarian life.

I stayed at Michael Grillmair's flat in the village of Petershausen and got to meet a lot of people. The introduction to Barbara and Sebastian Pfab (Dieter's parents) was particularly interesting. They lived in the tiny hamlet of Ziegelnobach and were, for all intents and purposes, ordinary Bavarian citizens, except that they were to become anything but ordinary to me. Over the following years they would welcome me into their home and treat me as one of their family.

Sebastian Pfab was particularly receptive to me and after a while it became obvious that he looked upon me as some kind of surrogate son. The feeling was mutual, and I respected him as a father figure. Communication between us had its difficulties, as his English was almost non-existent and my skills in the German language were at the beginner's stage, but I would return to Bavaria every year for the next 25 years. A chance meeting had turned into a minor passion for that particular region of Germany. The many different adventures I have enjoyed during my times there could fill a book many times over. They also served as a reminder to me that in every nation there is inherent good.

Two years later, in 1987, a newspaper article appeared in the local press which was to prove invaluable in the years ahead. Since my discovery of my mother's correspondence and my father's wartime photograph there had been long a period of inactivity on my behalf. I felt that I had a real mystery on my hands, and did not have a strategy or means to solve it.

The newspaper story was all about a new voluntary organisation called the Transatlantic Children's Enterprise (TRACE). It had been set up by a group of like-minded people chaired by the well-known writer Pamela Winfield. All these people had a common link - they were the British children of World War II GIs, or had American husbands/wives who were seeking to find their biological fathers. By collectively establishing contacts and links, an established plan of action and information resources had been devised.

I decided to write to them and ask for a membership form. It came back almost straight away, and very soon I became a fully paid-up member of this self-help organisation.

The return letter confirming this did not reveal any new information, but emphasised the fact that I was not alone. There were hundreds, if not thousands, of people in a similar situation, and we all had to make a personal effort to help ourselves. This was sound advice, and along with it came other snippets of information containing addresses to write to, protocol to follow, people who might assist and some past success stories.

From the information provided I wrote to the National Personnel Records Center (NPRC) in St Louis Missouri. I gave them the few details I had, and waited.

It was some weeks before a response came through, and it proved to be yet another negative result. The authorities simply stated that they had no record of a Joseph Schwartz/Schuranty from the town of Ann Arbor who had served in the US military during the time of WWII, and could I therefore supply them with more facts. How could I supply more facts when all I had was a photograph, and inscription and an address? This was demoralising.

I wrote to the President of TRACE, Pamela Winfield. In her reply to me I was told that Ann Arbor was quite a wealthy town and that it had a large university there. Suddenly I had an inspiration. My father had referred to "this institution" in one of his letters. Could this be the university at Ann Arbor?

My next move was to obtain the address of the university, which bore the rather grand title of the "University of Michigan", indicating that it was an institution of some importance. I duly wrote to them asking if they had a record of student Joseph Schwartz/Schuranty attending there in the immediate post-war period. Many weeks then passed with no reply, and I decided to write to another of the contacts that TRACE had sent me, the secretary of the 410th Bomb Group Association, Ed Dionne, who lived in Olympia Fields, Illinois. In my letter I introduced myself, gave what little detail I had about my father and asked for his help.

Ed sent back a long reply telling me all about himself and his wartime experiences in England, and was enthusiastic about helping me. This proved to be the beginning of several exchanges of correspondence with Ed and his wife Colleen.

Ed's first reply told me that he had been a staff sergeant aerial gunner stationed with the 9th Air Force 410th Bomb Group based in England at Gosfield, Essex. He had flown many missions during WWII and told me of the great comradeship and appreciation of the local people he had experienced during those times. Ed had spent many hours trying to make some sense of the limited information available and described himself as my personal "detective". After drawing many blanks, he came up with a plan to make the long journey to Ann Arbor and make some discreet enquiries on my behalf.

It never happened. During this time Ed had been attending the famous Mayo clinic for treatment of a severe diabetic condition. In early November 1988, I received a letter from Colleen Dionne. She told me that she had gone to bed at the usual time leaving Ed (who was a night owl) watching television. In the morning she found him still in his favourite chair – he had passed quietly away. My chance of meeting him in person and also maybe a chance of solving the mystery of my father also slipped away that night.

Over in America in the early 1990s, new legislation had been passed easing the privacy levels imposed by the military on access to WWII soldier records, so now seemed the right time to write to the NPRC once again in the hope that new information would come to light. However this new hope was quickly dispelled when a reply came back in the same negative format as the previous ones had.

This repetition had the effect of making me think more laterally. Perhaps a US genealogist could uncover some information which would lead me to my father. Apart from the fact that he had been in the war, the only other relevant details were two addresses in Michigan.

Joanne H. Harvey was a professional genealogist based in Lansing, Michigan. I wrote to her, enclosing the introductory deposit fee, and her reply included a number of detailed questions. To undertake a search for my father she would need answers to these. The letter concluded by telling me that the university in Ann Arbor was "big on secrecy". She herself had applied for the records of her deceased father-in-law and been refused!

I wrote back to Joanne to tell her that I was very sorry but I could not add anything to the information I had already given her. She wrote back, returning her fee and suggesting that the best course of action would be to search for a record in St Louis, Missouri of a marriage between Joe Schwartz (or Schuranty) and a Mary. To do that she thought it would be more practical for me to use a genealogist who actually lived in that city and recommended contacting Dr Chris Nordmann. I decided to engage his services and sent the brief details I had, together with the requisite fee.

In his reply Dr Nordmann said that he could find no record of such a marriage around the post-war years. He mentioned the possibility that the ceremony might have taken place in another state.

The TRACE newsletters were constantly giving details of successful searches for missing fathers, but this did nothing to boost my morale. Once again I suspended my search.

One of the chief motivating factors in my search was the fact that "Joe" had mentioned that his new wife in St Louis had been expecting a child. If that was the truth, then there would be a half-brother or sister somewhere in North or South America. I felt an almost overwhelming desire to meet these people and see what similarities existed, along with a first-hand account of what my father really was like to live and grow up with.

Indeed the speculation extended to the moment I would get to meet "Joe" for the very first time. I envisaged that some kind of formal discussion would have to take place during which I could give him the opportunity to explain the reasoning behind his total rejection of me and the abandonment of his responsibilities towards my mother.

There is no doubt that this discussion would, in all probability, have been conducted with some vigour on my part and, it is fair to say, some forceful criticism. From my father's point of view it would definitely not have been a "walk in the park". Notwithstanding this, the fact would have remained that he was indeed my biological father and had the right not only to reply to criticism, but also to command the respect normally afforded to a father.

The 1990s were now in full progress, and so were my annual visits to Bavaria to meet up with the friends I had made in Corsica. By now I had become a familiar visitor in the village of Steinkirchen, where I participated in the twice-weekly football training sessions at the local club, SpVgg Steinkirchen. The village itself was in pleasant countryside but nevertheless not on the radar of any prospective tourist. These visits usually took place in September, around the same time as the annual Oktoberfest beer festival in the city of Munich.

During my times there I went to many of these festivals, but one particular one had an unexpected effect on me. It was the usual scenario on this particular day - the "oompah" band playing on the rostrum, the beer tent tables overflowing with beer and food, tourists and locals all engaged in a semi-drunken frenzy of enjoyment. That is no exaggeration. Together with the attractions of an adjoining fairground, it is simply a celebration of happiness.

I decided that I needed a break from this euphoria and left the tent for some fresh air.

As I walked along past the rows of beer tents and fairground attractions, a sudden feeling of anger invaded my senses. I found myself in a rage about my father, and over and over again I kept thinking about why he had apparently abandoned us, even though he knew my name and that I was his son. I actually felt as if I wanted to hit someone. This was totally out of character for me. This emotion kept spinning around my head for several minutes before I regained my composure and returned to the festivities.

This brief experience brought the realisation that what had transpired in the past had affected me more than perhaps I cared to admit. Maybe in the future I would have to make a greater effort to solve things and put it all behind me.

CHAPTER EIGHT

FALSE TRAILS AND DASHED HOPES

Sometimes when I made my annual trip to Bavaria, the journey meant a change of aircraft at Charles De Gaulle airport, Paris. In the terminal there I could capture a brief image of the city in the form of souvenirs, fashion and the café menus. I now wanted to experience for myself the city about which my father had written to my mother in early 1945.

In 1991 I visited Paris for the first time. I did the usual sightseeing - Eiffel Tower, Champs Elysées, Arc de Triomphe, Sacre Coeur, Pantheon, etc. The timing of my visit coincided with a prominent date in European history - May 8th, VE (Victory in Europe) Day.

The event is celebrated with style in the French capital. The ceremony of laying a wreath on the tomb of the unknown soldier at the Arc de Triomphe is attended by the President and leading foreign dignitaries. This is preceded by a parade of WWII motorbikes and vehicles. At the end of the ceremony a full military parade is conducted from the Arc and along the Champs Elysées. All the Allied forces are represented, and it is a magnificent display of co-ordination and unity. Standing alongside the many spectators, I felt enthralled by the spectacle.

After the celebrations, wanting to experience a more authentic side of the city, I rode on the Metro to some of the lesser-known suburbs. Taking this "off-tourist" approach meant that I could observe everyday Parisian life and take a drink in an authentic bar. Back in the war years, before the city was liberated, it would have been more restrictive.

While I could get lunch at a restaurant of my choosing, I remembered what my father had written to my mother in one of his letters:

Was in Paris recently and the food situation there is critical, even worse than England. An American or British soldier cannot be served in a civilian restaurant. Thank God that there were several Red Cross clubs and NAAFIs where you could get a bit of lunch.

This letter had no date on it, but it must have been written after August 25th 1944, the day Paris was liberated from the occupying German military.

While there were still many parts of Europe I wanted to explore, America hadn't been entirely forgotten. In 1997 the *South Wales Echo* newspaper published a letter from an American, Matt Fortney, who had been stationed in Caerphilly for six months in 1944. 53 years on he wanted to revisit some of his old haunts. Normally a letter like that would have aroused only a passing interest in me. However, Matt was from Michigan and perhaps he and his wife Helen could tell me more about the state from which my father had written to my mother in 1946. Nothing ventured, nothing gained. I wrote to him.

In his reply he told me he had many happy memories of

Caerphilly as a soldier in the 634th Quartermaster (Laundry) Company. After all these years he had suddenly felt an overwhelming desire to come back to the scene of part of his youth. In particular he wanted to see again his then girlfriend, Joan Evans, with whom he'd re-established contact.

After we had exchanged several letters, I invited the Fortneys to come and stay with me. They gratefully accepted and were scheduled to arrive on a Bank Holiday Monday in late August. After getting home from work that day I settled down to await their arrival. The light was fading when the doorbell finally rang. A taxi-driver with a quizzical look on his face was standing in my drive.

"Mr Spencer?"

"Yes?"

"I have some Americans for you. Is that OK?"

"Yes!"

Only when the formalities had been completed did I realise why he was slightly apprehensive. The Fortneys had, or so it seemed to me, brought all the luggage in Michigan State with them. I lost count of the number of cases that came out of the taxi, but an entry in the Guinness Book of Records could not be discounted! Somehow we managed to find space for all of them inside what now appeared to be a very tiny two-bedroomed bungalow.

Although I was still working, I managed to show them some of the local landmarks and attractions. Of more importance was Matt's reunion with Joan, which was quite an emotional moment for both of them.

Another moment was when all four of us went to her parents' grave in the nearby village of Rudry, in the churchyard there. When we came to leave, Matt broke down in tears. He remembered how Joan's parents had treated him like a long-lost son and had been very sorry when he had had to leave Caerphilly and go to the French mainland.

Years later I went back to the graveyard. In the intervening years Joan had passed away and been buried beside her parents.

On the last day of their visit, Matt wanted to have his picture taken in front of Caerphilly Castle, at the very same spot where he had stood in 1944 as a young man of 21. We had only a 53-year-old monochrome photo of Matt in his uniform to guide us as we tried in the fading light to locate the exact section of the castle green, with its background of battlements and towers. But just as the light was beginning to go, we found it and I took the photo that meant so much to him.

When Matt got back to Michigan he converted my colour photo to monochrome and sent it back to me, together with a copy of the 1944 image. In the accompanying note he wrote: "Here's my black and white version. When comparing it with the 1944 photo, I couldn't help but notice how much the castle had aged. I, of course, haven't".

The visit had been a great success all round. I might not have learned a lot about Michigan, but I'd found two new friends.

Shortly before their departure, it was announced on the radio that Princess Diana had been killed in a car crash in Paris. In a bizarre way this tragic event will, for me, always be associated with the Fortneys' visit.

Later that year they invited me to visit them in the summer of 1998. Two weeks before I was due to fly out that August I went to watch a local league football match. Standing behind the goalmouth, I watched some local lads having an impromptu pre-match practice. Suddenly the ball came flying in my direction. My reactions were perfect - I caught the ball cleanly and returned it to play.

The lads expressed approval of my dexterity, but I knew that I had not caught the ball cleanly. One of my fingers was beginning to throb, and the pain would not go away.

The next day I visited the local hospital, where they examined my hand. I was told to come back a week later for a final check. When I did so it was clear that something was wrong. An X-ray revealed a fracture in my finger, and within 12 hours I was on the operating table having it pinned.

I was stunned to learn afterwards that it would be eight weeks before sufficient healing would take place to enable me to return to work. My journey to Michigan was just around the corner, but the surgeon assured me that it would be possible to travel over. However any driving would be out of the question, so I would have to rely entirely on the assistance and generosity of Matt and Helen.

They were there to greet me when I landed at Traverse City airport. Matt took my picture as I emerged from the arrival gate. It was flattering and humbling to have such attention. We then called in at the local radio station to meet their disc jockey son David. Then we were on our way to the semi-rural setting of East Jordan. I spent a wonderful 10 days with Matt and Helen, and they drove me everywhere to see the sights.

Halfway through my visit I decided to tell them what my true connection with America was, and my story was received with great interest. Helen was particularly enthralled, as she had attended business college in Ann Arbor after the war and was able to describe the city and neighbourhood to me. She wondered if perhaps my father had tried to find my mother and me in later years, but had failed because of our many changes of address. I'd never really thought of that possibility, but I couldn't help thinking that he could have eventually traced us had he really wanted to.

My holiday over, I returned home to Wales and eventually to working life in the paper mill. During my long absence a vacancy among the shift electricians had come up. Their rota involved working two twelve-hour days, followed by two twelve-hour nights and then four days off. After a period of eight weeks there would be an eighteen-day break. This annualised hours rota of time in and out of work was mandatory without additional holidays, which meant complying with it for the entirety of 1999.

In order to select a replacement person the names of all the day electricians were placed in a hat and the successful candidate drawn out. Lo and behold, my name was drawn. Like it or not, a year of 12–hour day/night shift working, which was something I hated, lay ahead of me. I did put forward the theory that every ticket in the hat had had my name on it, but it was to no avail!

Four months into 1999 there came the unexpected announcement that the mill would cease production by the end of the year, and everyone would be made redundant. Although I had worked there for 26 years, I wasn't sad to go. The working atmosphere had changed over the years, which was symptomatic of the increased demands in world markets. In any event the redundancy terms were more than reasonable. On the other hand, my chances of finding a similar job at the age of 54 were limited and would require a more flexible approach to what vacancies existed.

After several interviews and applications, all of which resulted in nothing, I took a temporary part-time job in a Cardiff department store. Eventually I returned to my trade and worked for five and a half years as an industrial electrician for a Bridgend company which outsourced me on short term contracts. This time in my working life proved to be an interesting and challenging time for me and involved a lot of travelling and working in many different offices and factories. After being in one place for 26 years, it was a new experience and a chance to meet new people.

Ironically the job had not come my way through advertising or Job Centre posting but by word of mouth from a former paper mill colleague!

All this had the effect of diverting my attention from the search for my father, but this lapse was only a temporary one. One evening I happened to be going through some old documentation and suddenly realised that I had not renewed my membership subscription to TRACE (Transatlantic Children's Enterprise) for some considerable time. I felt a little guilty about this and hastily sent off my renewal fee to the secretary.

Very shortly afterwards I began to receive a series of telephone calls from a fellow TRACE member, a lady called Rhonda England. Rhonda, the daughter of a GI, had traced her father via TRACE and wanted to help me. She felt that I should write again to the National Personnel Records Center in St Louis. She emphasised that I had a right to try to identify my father and said that recent legal actions in the US had made it much easier for people like me to do so.

Encouraging as her message was, I personally wasn't hopeful, since all my previous attempts had ended with St Louis returning my application and stating that they had no record of a Joseph Schwartz from Ann Arbor. They had always asked if I had his service number, and my answer always had to be no. They had equally routinely informed me that in 1973 a fire had destroyed all military records from surnames Hubbard to Z.

Having enthusiastically adopted my cause, Rhonda came up with a list of eight Joseph Schwartzes now living in Michigan

State who, like my father, had been 25 or 26 in 1946. I decided to write to each of them.

At the end of several weeks I'd received only one reply. Perhaps a call to those who hadn't would produce better results? It didn't. The answers I got were either that the person I was calling had not served in the military at all or that he had served only in the US or the Pacific Theatre.

When I called one particular gentleman, Joseph C. Schwartz of Saginaw, Michigan, he slammed the phone down with the words "I think, sir, that you are a salesman. Goodbye".

Rather than call again and invite the same response, I wrote explaining my purpose in calling him using the usual format of "looking for a long-lost friend of the family from the time of WWII". He replied by post almost immediately, apologised, and invited me to call him back right away. I did. We had a most pleasant conversation. Unfortunately he had served only in the Pacific theatre.

Because this man's reaction had so impressed me, I felt that I could tell him the true reason for my enquiry. Both he and his wife Betty were sympathetic and wished me every success with my search. They were, it has to be said, none too impressed by the way my father had behaved towards my mother and me after the war.

During the brief few years that followed our initial contact, I had many delightful conversations with Joseph C. Schwartz. Joe always told me that he was the talker and that Betty was the writer - indeed she wrote several nice letters to me over the short time I knew them. It is to my eternal regret that I never got to meet this wonderful couple; Joseph passed away before I could fulfil that ambition.

At the end of what proved to be our final telephone

conversation he said something that will remain in my heart forever. In closing he said: "Norman, I'm not your father, but I wish I was". For once I could not think of a suitable reply. I simply thanked him for his sentiment and bade him goodbye, little knowing that it was for the last time.

By now the search had lost some momentum and yet another letter to the University of Michigan had yielded no response. By this time Rhonda England was, I think, equally frustrated by our lack of success, and in truth weary of my telephone calls. She effectively announced that for her the search was at an end. Her opinion was that I would now never find my father and instead should accept that Joseph C. Schwartz had effectively given me "unconditional love".

For that I should be eternally grateful. It goes without saying that I am. I am grateful to Rhonda too for all her efforts on my behalf. But somehow I felt that I could not accept this latest setback, even though it seemed on the surface to be the end of the line. I refused to believe that after serving in the military, attending university and even getting married, my father had not left some kind of traceable footprint on this earth.

I directed my attention to the typewritten letter in which he had informed my mother of his forthcoming marriage and emigration to South America. Where in that vast continent would a US citizen be likely to go?

This really was looking for a needle in a haystack. I called the St Louis Public Library and enquired if any of their staff had knowledge of immediate post-war business connections between that city and South America. They gave it some thought, but could not point to anything definitive. I thanked them for their time and trouble and went back into a slightly defeatist mode. I had visited this scenario many times before.

Time ticked by once more, and I made sure that my membership subscription to TRACE was kept up to date. But now something had come into the equation which was to change the whole aspect of my search. I had become a member of the "internet generation". I was on-line, on-message, on-email and ready to open a new chapter of exploration and learning. The world had become a village.

One of the first emails I received was from the secretary of TRACE, Norma-Jean Clarke-McCloud. She had been re-reading my details on my membership file and had listed a number of relevant questions about the progress of my search. Included in these questions was a request for copies of everything the NPRC had sent to me. This awakened the energy I needed to continue. It ended with the line: "Come on Norman, don't let anything beat you! Best wishes from a kindred spirit – Norma-Jean. "

From past TRACE newsletters I knew that Norma had herself managed to find her GI family in California after many years of blind alleys, mistaken identities and discouraging comments. It was my good fortune that she happened to cast a look over my details and had glimpsed possible ways forward.

The next year, 2009, looked brighter already. Now, with the aid of my laptop, I could communicate much faster than with conventional mail and increase the chance of a swift reply. I looked up the website of the public library in Ann Arbor where, by the address on his WWII photo, Joe had apparently resided. I had already written to 703 Church St there, also to the mysterious West Lodge address in the neighbouring town of Ypsilanti. Both enquiries had been ignored, for what reason I did not know.

Now I sent a request to the library and attached a scan of

the wartime photo. They very quickly conducted a search on my behalf and provided me with a list of potential candidates from the area. Alas, as so often before, the men on their list either didn't fit the criteria or had already been eliminated. The library even took the time and trouble to look for any record of a marriage between a Joseph Schwartz and a Mary somebody. No record could be found.

Maybe I was looking for the wrong man? I began to wonder again whether the inscription on the photo might be Schwarty or Schuranty, even though my step-grandmother in Sheffield had assured me that my father had been called Schwartz.

As luck would have it, a week or so later, purely by chance, I came across an old shopping list that my mother had written. Suddenly it dawned on me. The handwriting on the back of the photograph was not, as I had assumed, that of Joseph Schwartz. Comparison with the shopping list indicated that it was my mother who had written the name and address on the back of the photo!

Placing the two examples side by side, it quickly became obvious that the surname was indeed Schwartz. A vital piece of information had finally been underscored. Now I could move forward again with increased confidence.

My thoughts turned yet again to the University of Michigan. If, as seemed likely, my father had studied there, then surely there had to be some record of his attendance and possibly even a graduation photo.

I called the University and was put through to the library/records department. They promised to carry out some investigations. Around a week later I called them back. Sorry, there was no trace of a Joseph Schwartz from circa 1946. Nothing at all.

This was another moment of frustration. Just as it seemed I was homing in on a solution, it was dead stop. I thought back to 1988, when the late Ed Dionne had told me that my father must have been in the 9th Air Force. He worked this out because Joseph had written to my mother from France.

Latterly I had found several books in the local library about the United States Army Air Force in WWII. One in particular was entirely dedicated to the 9th. From what I read in this book, I imagined that my father must have been an aircrew member in one of the heavy bombers. These Boeing B-57s were known as "flying fortresses", and I had visions of him engaged on a daytime bombing mission over the heart of Germany while coming under heavy anti-aircraft fire. Perhaps my elusive father had been a real wartime hero?

CHAPTER NINE

THE ELUSIVE
JOSEPH SCHWARTZ

After yet another military record enquiry had drawn a blank, the National Personnel Records Center in St Louis took the unusual step of sending me a "spreadsheet". This came through the post in the form of six foolscap sheets, together with specific instructions for how to tape the sections together in order to produce a readable format.

When assembled, the spreadsheet provided me with a list of the basic military details of no fewer than 125 Joseph Schwartzes who had served in the Army and Air Corps during World War II. This looked to be extremely helpful, but, just to dampen things down a little, a handwritten note in the right-hand column had the inscriptions: "These are all the WWII Army+Air Force Soldiers (+/-)… There are none from Ann Arbor Michigan". Which meant there was no entry of a Joseph Schwartz from Ann Arbor.

In spite of this emphatic statement, I proceeded to check through the roll call and sift out the most likely candidates. The year of birth was a major factor here, along with marital status, branch of the military and education. What the list did not indicate however was which Theatre of Operations the listed soldier served in. So, although it was technically possible to have served in both European and Pacific Theatres, clearly the European case would be the most likely one to pursue.

With the help of Norma-Jean I wrote off to the military requesting details of the two most likely candidates. Subsequent replies on these revealed that the soldiers concerned "Served USA only". This was something that I had not considered before.

Looking at my father's photograph for the umpteenth time, I had managed to come to the conclusion that he might have been a navigator. It was not a razor-sharp image, but the metal badge on his tunic seemed to indicate either a navigator or observer.

Sometimes you can jump to conclusions without positive proof of things. Once some time has passed, they assume the status of cast-iron facts. When Norma-Jean sent an email asking if my father was a navigator, I immediately told her he was, without stopping to think that this was only a theory.

Norma had uncovered an obituary relating to former WWII USAAF Navigator Joseph Morris Schwartz of Baltimore, who had flown 31 missions in Europe. We decided to write off for details of his military service, in the hope that this might be the elusive Joseph Schwartz my mother had known.

The obituary had stated that Joseph Morris Schwartz had married shortly after the ending of hostilities. Post-war, he had set out doing a labouring job and gone on to develop a successful property business in Baltimore.

My curiosity was aroused by this discovery. From several internet searches it became clear that this man had been more than a little successful. He had become a multi-millionaire, passing away on November 14th 1999.

Then I discovered a newspaper report telling of his $6 million donation to a Baltimore hospital. The report included a picture of him and his wife Corrine.

This Joseph Schwartz had married in 1946. His first business venture had failed, but after this he had established a successful property building empire. My heart sank when I read this, for although the search for my father was a necessary and natural thing to do, I definitely did not want to find that he had become a millionaire. I would have been perceived as some kind of legacy shark.

Was the obvious success of Joseph Morris Schwartz the same "success" that my father had speculated on while writing from West Lodge Ypsilanti/Ann Arbor? The possibility that Joseph Morris Schwartz might be my father had to be explored in order to either eliminate him from my list of candidates or, just possibly, confirm him.

This did nothing to underline the possibility that this was the man I was seeking. The obituary had listed three surviving children, two daughters and a son. I decided to attempt to make contact with the son, Richard, in Baltimore and wrote a letter of enquiry using the usual "former wartime friend of my family" format.

A webpage article about Joseph M's philanthropy was illustrated with a 1980s image of him together with his wife Corinne. I printed the image, compared it with the wartime photo of my father and saw several similarities, despite the time lapse of some forty years.

My good friend and neighbour Eiddwen Hudson has a good eye for detail, so, without divulging the true reason for my question at this stage, I asked her to compare the two photographs and then posed the question, "Do you think these two people are related in any way?" The answer came back, "Yes, I think so - they could be brothers".

I went away with the thought that Joseph Morris Schwartz had to be confirmed or eliminated before the search could move on. Several weeks went by without any reply. In contrast, the response from the National Personnel Records Centre was prompt. Joseph Morris Schwartz had served in the USAAF as a navigator on B-17 aircraft and had left active military service on November 7, 1945.

They provided another vital piece of information. He had returned to the US on August 19, 1944. If that were true, it ruled him out, since I had been conceived somewhere around the last week of December 1944.

I decided to telephone the Center and ask them to double check. Might he not have returned to the UK later? They could neither confirm or deny that possibility. Once again everything was up in the air.

The obituary had stated that Joseph Morris Schwartz had a son and two daughters, so in the light of a non-response from son Richard, a search was made and a "candidate" in Arizona, namely his daughter Roslyn Stoff, who now lived in Scottsdale, Arizona. I sent a "searching for a WWII family friend" letter to Arizona, and once again, the waiting began.

Also mentioned in the obituary were a friend of the deceased, Ron Creamer, and a Rabbi by the name of Ari Flamm. I compiled and posted a polite enquiry to these gentlemen asking for their help in my search. No responses were forthcoming, and I can only assume that these people had viewed my letters with suspicion and discarded them.

At the end of the day there was no obligation on their part to reply.

The obituary for Joseph had contained a colour photograph which seemed to have been taken some time in the seventies. Placing this image alongside the one my mother had kept all those years, the similarities could not be dismissed. Norma-Jean seemed to be more certain than I that this was our man, and advised me to "brace myself" for a conclusion of the search.

Acting on this basis, I did some telephoning of the high schools in Baltimore and managed to locate the very school Joseph had attended prior to WWII. The people at the high school were most helpful and, after locating a graduation year page complete with images, they promised to send over a copy.

It was no more than a week later when the copy arrived and with it came unexpected disappointment. The youthful image of the 18-year-old Joseph Morris Schwartz did not appear to resemble that of the Ann Arbor Joseph. It was hard to be precise in comparing an 18-year-old student to that of a person in his early 20s dressed in military attire. Nevertheless the identity of this man had to be positively ruled out by one of his surviving relatives or friends, and from this requirement the silence was deafening.

It was of little use simply to sit waiting. Having established that this man was definitely Jewish, I decided to contact the Jewish War Veterans in Washington and request that they place a "looking for" advertisement in their magazine newsletter. The only drawback was that no photographic image could be published. Nevertheless it was better than nothing, and it meant that yet another avenue was being tested during the seemingly endless wait for a response from Joseph's connections.

All this watching and waiting had the effect of increasing

my anxiety. There had been many instances in the past where TRACE members had, after years of searching, finally traced their biological father's identity, only to be told that he had passed away recently, sometimes only a few weeks earlier.

I still had the very strong feeling that the answer to this puzzle lay somewhere in the University of Michigan archives, so it was time to make contact once again. I called Caroline Shenks at the University Library and she promised to search their records for a Joseph Schwartz attending in the immediate post-war era. It was only a matter of a few days before a reply via email came through. There was no record of a Joseph Schwartz ever having attended or graduated from the university during that time. They had made a comprehensive search, and that appeared to be that.

While accepting this, and thanking the library for their good work, I could not believe that my father would not have left some kind of footprint somewhere. At this time there were several peripheral sources of information coming my way courtesy of the internet, and among them was a website dedicated to supplying replica WWII military badges.

I received a pleasant reply from the owner of this particular website who, by coincidence, happened to be a Mr Bob Schwartz. I emailed my father's wartime picture to him, and he replied saying that he had concluded that this person had a probable ranking of navigator, observer or aircrew member. The cap my father was wearing identified him as an enlisted man. Therefore, Bob concluded, he could only have been an aircrew member. This observation seemed to rule out the possibility that my father had been an officer of any description.

An English-based WWII expert, Bob Mynn, gave me another possible lead to investigate. He produced the name of a former USAAF soldier who had a large database of former personnel and had been a useful contact in the past. This gentleman was called Nevin Price, and I duly set to work in establishing contact with him. After forwarding the outline details of my research it was not long before I began conversing with Nevin on the telephone.

He analysed what I had told him and then came up with an unexpected piece of information. It was in relation to my father's time at the University of Michigan, and the fact that it seemed unlikely to be my father's home state. Nevin told me that a lot of enlisted men from the New England area had been sent to Michigan for pre-combat training. That could have been the reason why my father returned there after the cessation of hostilities.

This immediately prompted me to once again examine my St Louis spreadsheet and identify all the possible candidates from New England. It seemed that only three soldiers fitted the profile. I had agreed from the outset with Norma-Jean that our strategy vis-à-vis the NPRC would be for me to avoid bombarding them with all our enquiries - I would let her initiate some of them herself. She was, after all, vastly experienced in such matters. This time it was her turn to send off for details.

As sometimes happens in these instances, while various enquiries were being activated a written reply arrived from Roslyn Stoff in Arizona. It was a short but friendly response in which Roslyn carefully underlined the fact that the photograph of my father did not resemble her own father in any way. She wished me good luck in my search and was sorry that there was nothing more that she could do to help.

At first impression that appeared to be the conclusion of the matter, though in my mind there was still a slight feeling of doubt. Maybe the family were trying to cover up the real truth and suspected that I wanted access to their legacy. I needed to make 100% certain that this was not the case before moving the search on. I decided to call Roslyn Stoff in Arizona. As in the letter, she was a most pleasant and helpful person who managed to finally convince me that her family was not the biological contact I was seeking.

My attention now turned to Nevin Price's theory, and the three prospective candidates emanating from it. Eventually, after what seemed an absolute eternity, the replies came through from the NPRC. The replies were most revealing. One of the Joseph Schwartzes had unfortunately passed away in service back in 1944 and had never left the US. Another had been in the Navy, which effectively ruled him out, but the third candidate had indeed served in Europe, was in the Air Corps and was only two years out of the projected age group. Joseph E Schwartz had a Connecticut home address and had been in the UK for at least part of WWII. His "mustering-out" signature on the final pay docket looked familiar. I compared it over and over again with my father's writing and thought I recognised several matching traits. Signatures are not however the same thing as letter writing, and tend to be more flamboyant.

It was time to ask several trusted friends to examine and compare the material available. My friends' verdicts were marginally in favour of the signature and letter emanating from the same person. This heightened my anticipation. It was worth a try, so I sent the usual letter and my father's photo to Joseph E. Schwartz's current address in Sharon, Connecticut.

While I was waiting to see what this letter produced, completely out of the blue an email from Norma-Jean offered me a new approach. A journalist at the *St Louis Post-Despatch* newspaper, Susan Weich, had contacted Norma looking for information for a forthcoming feature about "GI war babies". Susan wanted to compile the article in time for publication on Father's Day, which was very appropriate. More to the point, it would appear in St Louis - the very city my father had written from, telling of a new love and marriage and saying farewell to my mother.

I made contact with Susan Weich and she interviewed me over the phone. It was over in an instant, with the promise of publication on Father's Day.

The written word can often come across with a totally different meaning from that of the spoken, devoid of emotion and nuances of meaning. So after explaining to Susan the circumstances which had led to my desire to find my father and the different emotions surrounding it, I was left with a very apprehensive feeling about going public with my story. I wondered what the reaction to it would be like.

With more free time on my hands than ever before, I took a brief holiday back in north-east Essex. This was the scene of my schooldays and my first workplace. I had managed to track down an old schoolfriend, John Breadman. He had lived with his parents in one of the estate houses on Holfield Grange, just outside the town of Coggeshall. John's father, William "Billy" Breadman, had worked as a handyman on the 3,000 acre estate for many years and had always been very supportive of my mother. John and I had attended the local secondary school together and he knew my mother from her time working as a cook at Holfield Grange. He was still living in the same area of Essex and remembered me and my mother fondly. After a reunion meeting with John I conveyed the story of the search for my father to him and he became very enthusiastic about the details revealed.

Some weeks later I received a call from him. He had been listening to a late-night phone-in on BBC Radio Norfolk. The topic on this particular evening was about people who had GI fathers, and listeners were invited to contribute. My curiosity was aroused by this news, and I looked up the radio station's website. A future daytime programme was planned for broadcast very shortly. I emailed them some brief details of my search and hopes.

Not long after the programme went out on air, I was put in touch with a lady living in Norfolk who was herself a "GI baby". Marilyn Kerton had grown up in rural Norfolk knowing that she was somehow different from the other children in her village school. Despite some unhappy experiences, she had grown up to become a valued citizen, with a good job and a nice family. When I made the call to her she made the type of sympathetic response you would expect from someone who had experienced similar emotions to myself. On hearing of my early years when the Prideaux family had made the offer of adoption and been refused by my mother, she made the remark: "Your mother must have been a wonderful, strong-willed person not to have given you up at that difficult time, how fortunate you were". This was truth personified, and music to my ears.

Marilyn concluded the conversation with words of encouragement: "You will find Joe, I just know that you will, he's out there somewhere, you have to believe that". On hearing that inspiring sentence, I bade her goodbye and promised to keep in touch.

My thoughts now turned to the pending arrival of Father's Day and the anticipated website posting of my interview with Susan Weich. The day duly arrived and it was time to check out the website of the *St Louis Post-Despatch*. Sure enough an article on "GI Babies" appeared, featuring a Mr John Wastle from Scotland, who had flown over specially to examine the hundreds of microfilm spools at the NPRC. Norma-Jean's own personal experiences in searching were also outlined in a brief summary, but there was no mention of myself and the story I had told the newspaper. This had to be a minor disappointment, though having my own individual search publicised by the media was never something I had actively sought.

I despatched an email to Susan Weich politely enquiring about the whereabouts of the missing article, and received an immediate automated reply. She was away on holiday! It seemed somewhat strange for a journalist to be away when an important article was due to be published, but it was just something I had to accept. The article was important to me, but to other people it was just a few lines on print or just another "scribing in cyberspace".

2009 was by now approaching the halfway stage, and I had been telling myself that this search, successful or not, had to have a finite end.

During my internet sessions I located the main newspaper for Ann Arbor, the *Ann Arbor News*. One particular item caught my eye. After a long and glorious history, the newspaper was to cease publication in July, though the on-line version would continue. I had often toyed with the idea of placing an advertisement in an Ann Arbor newspaper to the effect, "Does anyone know or recognise this WWII soldier? An old family friend from that time in London would like to re-establish contact."

There could be no more indecision on this, so I duly telephoned the newspaper. I outlined the content of the advertisement and made the appropriate payment. I told Norma-Jean what I had done and she approved of the idea. She also asked if I had included my email address in the advertisement. Being somewhat old-fashioned in my approach, I had not done this for fear I might be swamped by a lot of cranky responses. To correct this omission I made a deadline call to Trina Willis at the Ann Arbor News. The necessary email address was then added. Trina informed me that my advertisement would be published in 16 days' time, in the penultimate Sunday edition of the newspaper.

Finally an answer came through from Susan Weich in St Louis. Just before she had gone away on holiday an editorial meeting had decided that the Father's Day article had had to be trimmed. My article had been a victim of the cut. Susan apologised for the omission, but promised to publish the interview in the on-line edition of the St Louis Post-Despatch. The post appeared then duly appeared under the heading, "Can you help this man find his GI father?" and read thus:

I co-wrote a story one week ago about children of American GIs tracking their dads through the national Personnel Records Center in Overland. One account of a war baby I interviewed was not included in the article because of space issues, but I thought I'd post it here since he is still searching for his father, a man with a St Louis connection. Maybe someone can help him. Here's Norman Spencer's tale:

Spencer, 63, of Wales, knew nothing about his father until his mother Doris died in 1976, and he found letters in her personal effects that told of an affair with a U. S. Army Airman named Joseph Schwartz. In the first few letters, his father spoke mainly about his studies at a school in Michigan. He said he hoped to get a government radio operator's license and return to England. But a later letter gave details of something that must have broken his mother's heart, he said. His father wrote that a woman named Mary, the sister of an old schoolfriend, had come to visit, had gotten pregnant, and he was the father.

They got married and he was living in St Louis, learning his father-in-law's business. He said he would be going to work soon in the South American Branch. In the final paragraph he apologised. Tell Norman "some story of his father's death during the war or another story equally acceptable when he's old enough to understand" he wrote. He encouraged Spencer's mother to forget about him and marry an Englishman. But his mother never married and she moved from job to job as a cook. Spencer said that as a result he attended 10 different primary and secondary schools. If he did locate his father, he said he'd want to hear his side of things.

"I am angry but if I met him, I see no point in expelling my anger on him" Spencer said "You cannot alter the past".

Spencer does have his father's picture in uniform though, and he also has his dad's signature on those letters, so he can at least eliminate some of the Joseph Schwartzes.

"I don't want to spend the rest of my life obsessed with it but equally I wouldn't want to miss the chance of forming a contact because if he's true in what he's saying, I have at least one half-brother or half-sister over there," Spencer said.

Sure enough Susan had been as good as her word, and the text of my interview with her appeared in full alongside the only photograph I had of my father, the one with him wearing his USAAF uniform. This to me was of particular importance, for more often than not people cannot always recall a person's name from long ago. But a face is something that can lodge permanently in people's memories long after other recollections have faded.

I felt a real sense of relief that the contents of the article had been written in such a highly readable and professional manner and that everything contained therein was totally true and accurate.

July 12th was the day of publication in the Ann Arbor news. I wondered if someone would be opening their Sunday newspaper over there, reading my request and seeing the WWII photograph. Perhaps it would be his own photograph!

Over in St Louis the on-line article had produced two email responses, which was very pleasing. They were not from any former associates of Joseph Schwartz, but instead were from two ladies, Kathy Greifzu and Cheryl Sudbrock. Both these ladies resided in the St Louis area and were taken with my story, and both offered no-strings-attached assistance in locating my father. Naturally I contacted these two generous people and gave out all the relevant details and clues I had. Two more people at "home base" in America were now on the trail. The odds on my search succeeding had shortened!

At another level I was still a little uneasy about having the story of Joseph Schwartz, his pregnant wife Mary and their forthcoming emigration to South America broadcast, as it were, to complete strangers all across America and perhaps further afield. However, this reticence had to be counterbalanced by my desire to find my father. After all, he had been the instigator of my quest.

From Ann Arbor to New England, from Baltimore to Arizona and from St Louis to South America, this search had taken many twists and turns. In the midst of such uncertainty, more seemed destined to come.

My mother aged eight, with father George and stepmother Ethel

My mother aged 19

My mother aged 21

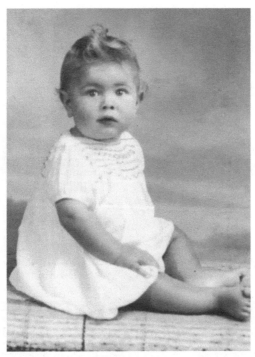

Hello brave new world! Me as a baby

Aged five at Hythe, Kent

Aged six, in my tank top

At West Hendred Primary School,
the Welsh dragon behind me

Aged nine and into books

Aged 10, complete with
Davy Crockett raccoon hat

Hamsell Lake House (a modern picture)

Holfield Grange, one of our Essex homes

The caravan at Leiston,
with my mother

Enjoying an ice-cream at
Clacton-on-Sea

The caravan at Leiston

The caravan at Pant y Waun

The caravan at Quakers Yard

My mother outside the caravan at
Quakers Yard, 1966

With my mother at the Watsons'
home in Honor Oak Park, London

Mother with Lesley Watson

With Arthur and Lesley Watson in Bognor Regis, 1978

At Caerphilly Castle, around 1970

Aged 21, at Cardiff
Pier Head moorings

The WWII photo I discovered in
my mother's personal effects

Joseph Schwartz
703 Church Street
Ann Arbor,
Michigan
U.S.A.

My father's graduation photo (left) and me.....You can see a likeness!

The Schwartz family in Altoona: Isadore, Philip, Leonard, Charlotte, Ruth

Leonard, Isadore
(my father) and
Philip Schwartz

The 'Terror of the Ozarks' crew, L-R – Staff Sgt Isadore Schwartz, Technical Sgt Douglas Mitchell, First Lt William Thompson, 2nd Lt Benjamin Campbell and 1st Lt Rollo Jacobs.

My father working at his radio station in Altoona

Marion and Walter Prideaux

First meeting with Aunt Marian, April 2011

Bruce and Charol Thompson

With LeAnn at Longwood Gardens, Pennsylvania, autumn 2012

My cousins Joshua and Adam Johns

Matt and Helen Fortney

My Californian cousins Paula, Joshua, Adam and Scott Johns

With Aunt Ruth, Carlsbad,
California, 2010

My Bavarian friends Barbara and
Sebastian Pfab

My father's grave in the San Fernando Valley

Ramsbury, England – standing on the spot where the 437th TCG radio operators' Nissen hut once stood. The inset photo shows my father on the same spot in 1944.

The author with an original WWII C-47 aircraft at Charleston US Air Base

437th TCG veterans (top to bottom) Tom Kilker, Paul Proulx and Ralph Carter
in the presidential suite of the Benson Hotel, Portland, Oregon

The veterans in Portland, 2011. Front row (left to right): Lewis Shank, Don Bolce, Paul Proulx and Dr Frank Morris. Standing: Tom Kilker, Lee Pennell, Bill Cheolas, Warren Halstead, Law Henderson and Vic Affatigato.

CHAPTER TEN

NARROWING
THE SEARCH

My search for Joseph Schwartz had by now become somewhat obsessive, and in my own mind perhaps a little too self-indulgent. Sometimes I would wake up at 4 am purely to check the inbox on my email system.

While the wait for the hoped-for responses to my Ann Arbor newspaper advert continued, my newly-established respondents in St Louis were about to hit the ground running. Kathy Greifzu and Cheryl Sudbrock were both very enthusiastic in their desire to help with the search, and had differing though equally viable strategies. Kathy's method was based on emotional intuition and personal interaction with anyone who she felt might provide the relevant information and who just might have an idea for a new and untried method of approach. Cheryl, in contrast, favoured a "can do" course of action. She immediately emailed everyone on my GI spreadsheet whose date of birth fitted my timeframe. Anyone who responded would then be mailed a letter containing a more detailed composition than that of the initial email.

Both approaches were both deeply appreciated by me and admired for their inventiveness and energy. This was not however a departure from the "seeking an old family friend from the time of World War II" method of communication, and it averted a possible rejection prompted by an over-enthusiastic and judgmental communication.

While all this extra activity was taking place, it was clearly no time for me to rest on my laurels. In particular the lack of response to my letter to Joseph E Schwartz in Connecticut had been playing on my mind. Something in my romantic subconscious had been giving me the thought that if this man from New England was my father then maybe, just maybe, he would sound just like former US President John Fitzgerald Kennedy. This was, of course, pure fantasy, but in a way it helped to relieve the monotony and tension of the search.

In any event, just as in the case of Joseph M of Baltimore, Joseph E of Connecticut had to be either confirmed or eliminated from the list of candidates. I made a search on White Pages and found what seemed to be his home telephone number.

I dialled the number. After what seemed an interminable amount of time, someone answered the call. It was the lady of the house, and after exchanging pleasantries and explaining the reason for the call I enquired as to whether they had received my letter and could they comment on it. The lady concerned was Mrs Eleanor Schwartz, and I can only say that she was politeness and charm personified, but when it came to answering a direct question she had the evasiveness of a politician. The conversation ended amicably with the request for me to "write again". It seemed a strange thing to say, but was better than being told to "go away".

During the entirety of the call there was no attempt to bring Joseph E. to the telephone, although it did seem that he was present in the house. I had a strong feeling that he was listening in to the conversation. I resolved to write again and, this time, to be a little more direct in relation to the true measure of my enquiry.

As a result of the help offered from Cheryl Sudbrock, emails were by now being circulated right across the length and breadth of the United States, all containing the same text:

I am seeking information on a Joseph Schwartz who was a US Army Airman during WWII. He served both in England and mainland France in 1944-45. He may have gone by the name of Joe at this time. During this time he became great friends with a family in London. Post-war he spent some time in the Michigan area attending college and they lost touch at this point.

If you would be so kind as to acknowledge whether or not this may be a relation you are aware of I would be very grateful. Any and all correspondence would of course be treated as confidential.

Cheryl's carefully-composed enquiry brought a few immediate responses, but all of them had one common factor - the sender confirmed that he was not a relation or had no knowledge of the person being sought. Then on July 15th a reply to my *Ann Arbor News* advertisement appeared in my email inbox:

Hello,
I saw your notice in the Ann Arbor News.

I do not know this man but would be willing to help you if I can. I am an adult adoptee who has made a similar search for family members.

I hope to repay in some way the kindnesses that were extended to me by perfect strangers when I was making my search.

Sincerely, LeAnn Fields.

Naturally I was delighted to receive this response and, although it did not appear significant at the time, the phrase "perfect strangers" was destined to become a constant theme from this moment in time.

The elimination process is often very tedious. When a "suspect" is finally eliminated, you often feel a certain amount of disappointment; at the same time you often heave a sigh of relief! That was my reaction when Cheryl Sudbrock sent me an email confirming that Joseph E of Sharon, Connecticut was definitely not the person I was seeking. It meant that I could move on to the next person or persons in line. Joseph E had telephoned Cheryl explaining that though he had served in England, it was definitely not around the time I was conceived. After providing this information, he had forgotten to replace the receiver, and for a while Cheryl was able to listen in to the private domestic conversation that followed between Joseph E, his wife Eleanor and the household dog!

Nothing earth-shattering came from this and Cheryl hung up after five minutes having found the ensuing conversation highly amusing and, I quote, "very Eastern".

Kathy Greifzu had uncovered another possible angle to the search. Joseph, in his final letter to my mother, had stated that he was "now in St Louis". Kathy had now uncovered the fact that in addition to St Louis Missouri there was a St Louis in Michigan State. The Michigan link had reappeared, and Kathy duly set about establishing contact with any historical or social societies which might exist in a small town in the heart of Michigan.

I had believed that the clue to unlocking this puzzle lay somewhere in the state of Michigan. Maybe this latest discovery would be the vital breakthrough. As if to underline this theory, my newspaper respondent LeAnn contacted me to tell me that she would be paying a visit to the Ann Arbor Library. There she would look up the post-war list of residents for 703 Church Street (the address on the back of the photograph) in the archive directories.

I was now trying to think of other possible things to investigate. If total strangers were now helping me, I should not sit idly by waiting for them to make a discovery.

I had a theory that if my father had studied at the University of Michigan under the GI Bill of Rights, then he would have had to apply for an educational grant of some description. Surely when he did this the relevant authorities would have required full details of his military service, employment record and home address. If this was true, then maybe some relevant paperwork might be still in existence.

With this this in mind I contacted the department of veterans' affairs in Washington. The man on the end of the line in Washington, Steve Westeveld, was neither dismissive nor enthusiastic about my enquiry. He promised to investigate further when time permitted. From the general tone of the conversation I didn't expect any immediate results.

My mind was already working overtime on the "Michigan connection" when an email with an attachment arrived from LeAnn. She had taken the time and trouble to drive past my father's post-war address and photograph the property concerned. Suddenly I found myself looking at a picture of the three-storey house with green shutters that was 703 Church Street, Ann Arbor. A myriad of emotions went through my mind while I was looking at this image. For the first time in my life I was looking at the house to which some of my mother's letters had been delivered, the same front door through which my father had gone in and out all those years ago.

Back then he had also used another address, West Lodge, Ypsilanti. Ypsilanti was the next-door town to Ann Arbor and was a key partner in providing student accommodation facilities for the University of Michigan. West Lodge had comprised a vast mini-city of prefabricated buildings which had been constructed to accommodate the wartime workforce at the massive adjacent Willow Run aircraft manufacturing unit. Following the cessation of hostilities, these buildings were adapted for the use of students attending the nearby University of Michigan in Ann Arbor.

It was to West Lodge that my mother's fateful letter had been sent in 1946 informing "Joseph Schwartz" that he was the father of a one-year-old boy in England. In his reply to my mother's news, Joe had replied that there was nothing he could do at that particular moment in time. He had gone on to say that there was one "ray of hope", and that was to the effect that he had good reason to believe that, as a result of his wartime aircrew occupation, he could apply for, and be granted, a radio operator's licence. Once that was obtained, he intended to seek employment on one of the many transatlantic ship companies, thereby making his passage back to England. All pure speculation at that moment in time, but nevertheless it was, as he stated, "a ray of hope". So after overcoming the initial shock of discovering his new status in the world, it appears that my father was considering a way to return to his wartime sweetheart and growing child.

My enquiries about possible "candidates" listed by the National Personnel Records Center were now, by process of elimination, beginning to dwindle, so it was now necessary to widen the sweep and include names of those soldiers born outside the estimated 1922 birthdate. One such possibility was

a Joseph B Schwartz, who came from Kendon, a town in
Kentucky near Cincinnati.

When I received a copy of this man's final pay check from
the authorities, it did not initially strike any great significance.
He had been born on 12. 12. 1920, a very near birthdate but
nothing more. What had awakened a real possibility was an on-
line newspaper article I happened to come across while reading
the *Ann Arbor News*.

I knew that in addition to writing from Church Street my
father had also corresponded from West Lodge, Ypsilanti. Nothing
particularly striking about that detail except that right now the
Ann Arbor News was featuring an article about the "Ypsituckians".
Apparently during the inter-war years a lot of people had
migrated from Kentucky to Michigan and to Ypsilanti, "Ypsi",
to work in the nearby Ford motor factory. To the present day, a
large "Ypsitucky" community has remained there.

Applying this piece of history to Joseph B. Schwartz made
me wonder if he was the Joseph Schwartz I was seeking. Perhaps
"Joe" was an "Ypsituckian" who had emigrated to Ypsilanti prior
to WWII. Then it would have been logical to assume that he
would have attended the university at Ann Arbor. It was almost
literally a stone's throw away!

From the tone of my father's correspondence, it had always
appeared that he had not originated from Michigan. Now,
however, a rational explanation seemed to be emerging, and it
was with great anticipation that I examined Joseph B's final pay
check. I couldn't decide if it was a perfect match for my father's
handwriting. Once again it was time to test my theory on some
friends and obtain their viewpoint.

First off was Norma-Jean in London, so I emailed the
signature for her perusal. Almost immediately the reply back was

in the affirmative. She could see several similarities between the signature and my father's handwriting. The score so far was 2-0, with myself and Norma in agreement.

Norma was if nothing else an ever-inventive lady with a keen eye for detail. During my search I had sent her an emailed a picture of myself at 14 years of age. An unexpected reaction came back down the line: "Norman, you do look very Jewish in the photo". I looked again at the photo and realised that this was an accurate observation.

Now it was time for another assessment of the Kentucky signature so, armed with the relevant paperwork, I went to visit a friend, David Jackson. I felt confident that he would merely underline the previous assessments, and then it would be plain sailing to contact this man and his family in Kentucky. After all, he had considerable experience in deciphering old manuscripts.

After meticulously examining the signature for what seemed an eternity, David concluded that he did not think Joseph B's signature on his pay docket matched my father's wartime letter handwriting. He went on to say that while nothing in this world is 100% certain, it would be a good idea to visit the city library and look up any books on graphology. Cardiff City library was my next port of call and, needless to say, there did not appear to be any relevant publications on the shelves that particular day.

The library attendant seemed to be have a free moment, so I approached him and asked for his opinion of the handwriting samples. To my surprise and, without any prompting, he said that in his opinion the signature and letters were written by the same person.

This was becoming a real roller-coaster, and I felt it was proving nothing. Signatures and handwriting are two different modes of communication and there are other influential factors.

One of the most salient is the mood of the person at the time of putting pen to paper.

I made an on-line search and located a graphologist in Scotland who was keen to help. I sent the relevant images for him to scrutinise and awaited the verdict. "Chairman of the jury do you find the defendant guilty or not guilty of the charges brought against him?" ...or words to that effect! This was my feeling as I opened the return email from Scotland.

It was a very detailed analysis of what I had sent and at the end of the script came the verdict: "It is extremely unlikely, as far as I can professionally tell, that the signature and the correspondence signature were written by the same person".

So of the five people consulted, the two people who could be classed as experts, David and the graphologist, had ruled against the signature.

All those years ago, from somewhere on the French mainland, my father had written, "When I am flying, pleasant thoughts and memories of you seem to filter into my mind which help to eradicate the horrible images of war which time can never heal". If nothing else my father seemed to have a certain level of sophistication in writing, and this seemed to be replicated in the very ornate signature of Joseph B. from Kentucky.

It was still necessary to eliminate or to confirm this man's eligibility, and with this in mind I sent the relevant details to Cheryl in St Louis in the hope that the present day address of him and his family could be located. I was also conscious of the fact that WWII veterans were passing away with increasing frequency. There had been several instances of people tracing their biological fathers only to find that they had been too late by a matter of months or weeks.

In the meantime Kathy had located a historical society in St Louis, Michigan. She had sent my father's photo and an accompanying article and this had been circulated among the society members. In all probability it would take a little time for any possible reaction to come through from this exercise.

With the Michigan theme very much in mind, I contacted the Alumni Association at the University of Michigan and made enquiries about placing an advertisement in their quarterly magazine. Their reply was systematic but not greatly practical. The advertising rates were prohibitive, circulation was limited and they could not include the wartime photograph. That effectively made that idea a non-runner.

My helpers and I had begun to assess the St Louis story about Joseph meeting Mary in Ann Arbor, the unplanned pregnancy and projected emigration to South America. To this end we began to search for a Joseph and Mary Schwartz in both the St Louis and Michigan state locations. A few possibilities did emerge, but in the end no definitive evidence was uncovered.

In the past some of my contacts had expressed doubts about the credibility of the whole story about Joe's claim to be marrying Mary. This was not something I wanted to contemplate. I did not want to go through life believing that my father had been so deceitful.

Back in Ann Arbor, LeAnn had been searching an on-line database for lists of obituaries relative to Joseph Schwartz born circa 1922. She also mentioned that some historical files existed in the archives of the University of Michigan Library under the auspices of the Bentley Historical Society. When time permitted she would drop by and ask to examine them, as they contained additional peripheral information over and above those of the Alumni Association.

Activity in the search was now at the highest level to date. It seemed the available options had all but been exhausted, so it became increasingly important to get a response from the family of Joseph Schwartz in Kentucky. He represented what was probably the last throw of the dice. From the Librarian at Kenton County Library I had obtained a likely current home address, which was near Joseph B's wartime address on his final pay check.

I duly wrote to him using the familiar format of enquiry and request for a response. The librarian, Jan Lester, was extremely helpful. So helpful in fact that she revealed to me that her own maiden name had been Schwartz, though she could not recall being related to the Kentucky Schwartz I was seeking. She then proceeded to run through a list of her relatives who, though not bearing the name Joseph, might have some recollection of a distant family member bearing that title. Unfortunately nothing came to light on this localised angle of enquiry, but it was nonetheless somewhat extraordinary to have chanced upon a member of the Schwartz clan in the midst of my contacts.

By now I was receiving weekly and sometimes daily feedbacks from my two volunteer assistants in St Louis. Steadily over time more and more little leads, more and more people and locations, were being systematically eliminated.

On the 29th October 2009, a letter arrived at my home. I could see from the sender's panel that it had been sent by a Paul Schwartz in Kentucky. With bated breath I opened the envelope. At last someone had bothered to reply in double-quick time, and I felt a great optimism.

This optimism evaporated in a few brief seconds as I began to read the first few lines of the correspondence. It had been written by Paul Schwartz, who introduced himself as the son of Joseph B Schwartz. Paul went on to say that he was sorry to inform me that his father was not the person I was seeking and that his father had served in the Pacific theatre of operations and had been deployed in Burma. To underline this fact he had kindly enclosed a wartime picture of his father in tropical military uniform. I could see straight away that there could not have been less resemblance between this soldier and Joseph Schwartz of Ann Arbor.

In their reply to my request for a copy of this soldier's final pay check, the National Personnel Records Centre in St Louis had stated that Joseph B had served overseas. They had not defined the exact theatre of operations where he had been involved. This was not an intentional oversight but more due to the fact that a disastrous fire in the building during 1973 had destroyed vast quantities of military personnel records. I now had to resign myself to the fact that on the face of it, this was as near a 100% confirmation of this man not being my father as you could possibly get.

I compiled a suitable response to Paul Schwartz, thanking him and sending my good wishes to his father, who was alive and well at the family home. I often used to picture the scene of an elderly American couple, well past retirement age, sitting happily at the breakfast table enjoying food and each other's company. Suddenly the mailman arrives with a letter bearing a UK postage stamp and the name of an unknown sender. The wife looks at the envelope and sees that it is addressed to her husband, but he asks her to open it. After briefly but slowly reading the correspondence, which also has a copy of an old WWII photograph attached, she passes the letter to her husband. He looks at it, appears to colour up slightly and falls silent. She then asks "What is all this about, and how come this person in the United Kingdom has your photo?"

That scenario had sat in my subconscious for some time, a little like the constant re-enactment of a dark comedy sketch, with the principal players being my father and the wife he allegedly married back in the post-war years. This family in Kentucky had been spared such a domestic drama.

Since my initial enquiry at the Department of Veterans' affairs in Washington, I had made several calls in the hope of receiving an update on the progress of their search for any relevant paperwork. Every time I made sure that I got to speak to the same person. I think this is essential in any format of customer request. My latest call got the same "we are still looking" response, but this time I sensed a marked lack of enthusiasm. It gave me the feeling that nothing was ever going to emerge from this particular institution.

The end of the year was by now fast approaching and the feedbacks from the "other side of the pond" were fast diminishing. It was time to review all the feedbacks I had received over the past two years from the NPRC in St Louis. These had been activated by my use of the spreadsheet showing 125 Joseph Schwartzes. At December 2009 it read thus:

Army Serial no. 12042622- Served in USA only

35673339 - Wrote to him - son replied with evidence that his father served in Burma and did not resemble the WWII J. S. picture.

19073685 - Served overseas but exact location (Europe/Pacific) is unknown.

13122379 - Served USA only

32572850 - Served USA only

12142850 - Served USA only

32651230 - Served overseas - location unknown - left service with rank of Private 1st class - New York address - died August 24th 2007.

11104099 - Deceased July 15th 1944.

11116454 - After several letters and phone calls, eventually established that this was not the person I am seeking.

13052867 - Served European theatre - born September 5th 1920 - Signature is "way out".

12090938 - Served USA only

19119603 - Served USA only

37399880 - Served Pacific theatre only.

13106531 - Served European theatre - returned to USA August 1944.

33467545 - Served overseas - exact theatre not known - obituary found - have written to son - awaiting reply.

Every request for information from the NRPC had been met diligently, and every result had been examined by me and followed up where applicable. Every resulting search had eliminated another individual from the search. I was beginning to think that the time was fast approaching when I would have to let to let Joseph Schwartz disappear forever into the mists of time. One thing was for sure. His picture had been circulated in more states, cities and towns than he could ever have hoped to visit in a lifetime!

Maybe, just maybe, 2010 would provide a vital piece of information and in turn reveal what really happened to my missing father.

CHAPTER ELEVEN

BREAKTHROUGH

The New Year of 2010 had been ushered in without any sign of a breakthrough, and everything was in limbo. However it was not long before another possibility was being pursued. LeAnn put forward a theory that if Joseph Schwartz had attended the University of Michigan, he would probably have become a member of the Alumni Association. She provided me with a link, and from this I duly despatched an email to Dave Richmond, the association's Advertising and Sponsorship Manager. I sent Mr Richmond the relevant details, sketchy as they were, of Joseph's estimated career at the University and the fact that I wished to contact his family. It was, of course, important that I appeared confident about the few details I had available.

Within 24 hours the answer came back that they had no record of a Joseph Schwartz. With this message Mr Richmond conveyed his best wishes for my continued search.

Although not exactly a body blow, this latest item of non-information only added to the frustration. I had the feeling that I was perhaps clutching at straws.

After this latest setback, I referred back to some of the past enquiries made to the NPRC. Looking through some of the final pay docket signatures, I located one which I had previously eliminated because the soldier was just outside the relevant timespan. With so many failures on record, the time had come to perhaps broaden the field of the search. Nothing ventured, nothing gained – this long shot did seem worth a try.

This particular Joseph Schwartz came from the city of Philadelphia. A quick check on Google Earth revealed that his immediate post-war address had been removed in favour of a new freeway! This meant I lacked the vital piece of information so often requested.

I contacted the Free library of Philadelphia, who had a section dedicated to "Ask a Librarian". This facility advertised a guarantee to reply within two working days. The answer to my query did indeed come through within the promised time, and it was to the effect that it was not possible for them to find Mr Joseph Schwartz of 5332 Claridge St Philadelphia. Unless I could provide details of the last known address, date of death (if applicable) and burial (if applicable) they could not assist. Should this not be possible, then they suggested I made contact with the Pennsylvania Genealogical Society.

Clearly to pursue this avenue of enquiry would involve more work than usual but, before I began to take up this challenge, something happened to divert my attention. Another email came through from LeAnn in Ann Arbor. Little did I know it at the time, but it would prove to be the starting point for a whole new series of discoveries.

She had come across a website describing the Bentley Historical Society, which had an archive library near the University of Michigan campus. Apparently this library held records of every student who had attended the institution, irrespective of graduation or grades. The only concern was the possibility that, in the wake of the huge post-war influx of returning GIs, publication of such records might have ceased or been suspended.

She promised that, when she next had sufficient free time, she would make a visit and inspect the archive files at Bentley. Her email had come through on January 28th, so it was with some surprise that I heard from her the following day and learned that she had indeed undertaken that course of action.

Reading through LeAnn's communication, it appeared that we had met yet another dead end. The Bentley Historical Society Library visit had revealed a complete run of student directories from 1944-50, one for each school year. However only one Joseph Schwartz had appeared, and that was for 1948-49 and 1949-50. This was clearly outside the relevant timeline.

She went on to say that she had discovered an entry listing an Isadore J Schwartz, an engineering student from Altoona, PA. He appeared in 1945-46 and again in 1946-47, and then disappeared completely. The question then arose - could Joseph have been my father's *middle* name?

LeAnn had then gone on to another stage and checked the WWII military enlistments which showed an Isadore J. Schwartz, born Altoona PA, enlisted on November 6, 1942. He was a high school graduate and a metal worker in civilian life. Height 71", weight 226lb. She concluded by saying that she knew I would be disappointed that we had not located Joseph, but she promised to make a visit to neighbouring East Michigan University and undertake a similar search.

So that was that, apart from the fact that the Isadore J. Schwartz statistics indicated that this person was a large, tall man and had served in the military during WWII.

I thought back to the sepia photograph discovered in my

mother's possessions; it was the image of a heavy-set man. My mind began to go into analytical mode and came out with the thought that maybe, just maybe, my father's first name was not Joseph after all.

The next communication from LeAnn did nothing to dispel this theory. Sensing that she was perhaps onto something, she had followed up the Isadore J Schwartz lead and on Saturday January 3, 2010 she consulted the 1930 census for Pennsylvania. She emailed me what she had found:

Schwartz, Philip, age 40, born Poland/Austria

Charlotte, age 35, born Poland/Austria

Ruth, age 11, born Pennsylvania

Leonard, age 9, born Pennsylvania

Isidore (sic) age 7, born Pennsylvania

Able, Nettie, age 60, servant

Parents speak Yiddish, came to the U. S. in 1904 and 1912 respectively and own a butcher's shop.

These people had all resided in the Pennsylvanian town of Altoona.

The moment I received this email, my mind set to work. From this information it seemed a reasonable assumption that the children of this household had been educated in the same town.

I quickly logged on to the internet, looked up "High Schools Altoona" and located the relevant telephone number. My thinking was that there must have been graduation ceremonies at this institution and perhaps some photographic records existed in the archives. This was indeed a very long shot.

In a very few minutes I got through to the High School in Altoona. A lady called Diane confirmed that there was a record of an Isadore Joseph Schwartz having attended the High School and graduated circa 1940. Diane read the details out to me:

"Newswriting Club, Physics Club, Academy of Science, 1, 2, 3; Intramural Sports 1, 2, 3; Mountain Echo Staff 1, 2. He was a busy guy. " However this was quickly followed by the words, "I'm sorry, but he is deceased".

Now I had to keep my composure and move onto the next enquiry. Would there possibly be a graduation photograph available within the archives? The answer to this was also in the affirmative. The lady on the end of the line emphasised that the photo was not exactly of modern-day quality and as such would not necessarily transmit well as an email attachment. She then said that the High School would be willing to post the details to me, so, after providing the details of my mailing address I thanked her kindly and prepared for a long wait. The call had lasted less than five minutes.

During the hours that passed by following that conversation. I reflected. If, as seemed likely, I had finally located my father, then the fact that he had passed away meant that the conversation I yearned for would not now take place. I would never be able to hear his explanation of times long since passed, nor would he be presented with my point of view on his actions.

My call to the High School had taken place on a Tuesday, and on the Thursday of that week I had been doing a little DIY in my kitchen and wondering if it would ever stop raining. Midday had ticked past and I had heard no sound of mail landing on my doormat, so it was with some surprise that I discovered a lone, somewhat damp, item of mail hanging from the interior letterbox flap. Closer examination revealed a US postmark and an "Altoona High School" logo. I opened the envelope and examined the contents, a single-sheet list of 24 students outlining details of their schooltime activities.

At the bottom of the page were cameo snapshots of them, accompanied by three blocks of eight names. Diane had attached a note:

"Isadore is the second one on the first column. Hope this is what you needed – Diane".

This was exactly what I needed!

My eyed moved across to the supposed image of Isadore. It was nothing like that of the wartime photo, not even allowing for the five to seven intervening years. My heart sank at the realisation of yet another wasted effort, and I put the page down.

A few moments passed and I picked it up again for another, final look. Suddenly it dawned on me that I had looked across the columns instead of down. Now I looked down the first column and found myself staring at an image which did have some resemblance to the wartime soldier, albeit without the military cap.

Could it be? Surely not. My mind wanted to believe, but at the same time I was highly sceptical. Could it really be true that in the last 72 hours this lifetime mystery had finally been solved?

Clearly I needed a second, unbiased, opinion and it was going to come from David Jackson. I called to check that he was at home, started my car, drove over the mountain and presented him with the Altoona High School page. He scrutinised it and then came up with the statement: "Yes, that's him. That's your father".

A simple statement, but one with profound significance. As I drove away from David's house those words kept repeating themselves in my head – "Yes, that's him. That's your father."

Now the full realisation of LeAnn's discovery in the Bentley historical archives began to hit home. In turn came the realisation that my mission to locate "Joseph Schwartz" over the past 34 years had been doomed to fail from its inception. The simple fact was, there had never been a Joseph Schwartz from Michigan State who was my biological father. In his place, an Isadore Joseph Schwartz from Pennsylvania had entered the frame.

Many past searches for GI biological fathers by TRACE members had been fraught with instances of errors made in the spelling of a surname, the misinterpretation of a name due to it being spoken in an unfamiliar accent, or simply because the man had lied about his family name or origin. I had become another victim of this type of anomaly, however unwittingly. Now I had to move on quickly and try not to chastise myself over making this basic error.

I sent the High School page to Norma-Jean the day it reached me. She had emailed a response to this new item of evidence. Norma, like David, felt certain that the High School picture was the same person as that in the wartime photo. The only difference was that my father had put on some "puppy fat" during his military service. Norma had not even followed Diane's instructions to identify the face by "looking down column one" but had used her own powers of observation and selected Isadore Joseph Schwartz straight away.

Now a third person needed to be consulted - LeAnn, who was in the very place where this had all began. I emailed the High School page to her and it was not long before a reply came through. It contained the word "Congratulations", and went on to say how thrilled she was that the long search was finally over.

The High School had told me that Isadore had passed away, so now I needed to establish exactly when, and if possible how. There had been many instances of people looking for their GI fathers having finally found them only to discover that they had recently died. For these people this had been both frustrating and heartbreaking, and I wondered whether I too would fall into this category.

Thanks to the wonders of the internet and the skill of LeAnn Fields, an answer very quickly surfaced. LeAnn located his death record in the California Death Index. It recorded that Isadore Joseph Schwartz had passed away on February 3rd 1966 – more than forty years before.

My reaction to this news was somewhat unorthodox. I realised that my father had missed out on seeing one of the greatest technological and logistic achievements of the 20th century, the successful Apollo 11 moon landing mission launched on July 16, 1969. This milestone event had been witnessed by some 500 million people worldwide. Had he lived long enough, there is little doubt that my father would have viewed this event at exactly the same moment as I had done. Father and son unknowingly in unison for the only time in their lives. Alas, this never came to pass.

Still to be found was my father's obituary, which I hoped would identify other family members with whom I could establish contact. I hoped that his premature passing had not been due to some violent act or horrible circumstance.

The *Altoona Mirror* website did not reveal any information on "Schwartz obituaries" but sometimes a call to the organisation concerned can be more productive. I made a note to call the newspaper the very next day. Looking through the list of reporting staff, I picked out one at random, William Kibler. I got through to William and began to explain that I had been looking for Isadore Joseph Schwartz, who was a good friend of my family from the time of World War II. This was not really a lie but simply another version of the truth, designed to avoid scaring off any potential contacts who might withhold vital information or clues. The late, great Pamela Winfield, founder of the Transatlantic Children's Enterprise (TRACE) had always advised exercising great caution when making enquiries about prospective family members and backgrounds, and this was not a time to stray from that well-proven philosophy.

William listened with interest to my brief explanation and said that if he could not locate an obituary for Isadore he would call around any remaining Schwartzes in the neighbourhood in the hope of locating a relevant one. He concluded with the observation that Isadore must have been very highly thought of for someone to want to contact him after such a long time.

Another possible way forward then occurred to me. Perhaps the public library in Altoona would have a city directory of residents from the immediate post-war period. The internet once again proved to be a real time-saver. I looked up the library telephone number and in no time at all I found myself speaking to a member of the reference department there. I explained that I was doing some research on a member of the Schwartz family, Isadore, who was an old family friend, and wondered if they had any present-day information on surviving family members. I provided them with the post-war address written in the Bentley archives, 1111, 18th Street.

I was asked to call back in around 20 minutes. When I called back a whole wealth of information about the Schwartzes was awaiting me. The librarian began to read out the information to me:

Father Philip had retired in 1957 and moved to Los Angeles, California, where he died in 1980. Mother Charlotte moved with him and died in 1973.

There were two daughters, Ruth and Marian. The librarian

thought that one of them must have been born after the 1930 census.

Ruth had married a man named Johns (by now my pen was going into meltdown trying to note down all that was coming my way) and moved to California in 1973. Marian had married a Garfinkel and moved to Philadelphia. Leonard had died in Altoona, aged 65.

There was no mention of Isadore, aside of a 1936 newspaper article which was not read out. Right to the very end the details of my father's life seemed determined to remain elusive!

Nevertheless the sheer speed and quantity of information that had been uncovered in just 20 minutes was breathtaking, and a great accolade to the people who had taken the time and trouble to research it so quickly. I thanked the library staff for their help, which was both considerable and considerate. They suggested that I should get in touch with the Altoona Historical Society, who met at the library on Saturdays.

My thoughts were drifting back to the date of my father's death. How had it come about that he had died at such a relatively young age? The adrenalin that surged at my discovery did not allow me to dwell too much upon this particular statistic. Under more normal circumstances I would have felt saddened and devastated at the realisation that, after all this, I would never get to meet my father, not now, not tomorrow, not ever.

I needed one more available piece of evidence to underline all that had been discovered. This was the signature on the final pay check. I contacted Norma-Jean and she quickly wrote off to the military records department in St Louis to ask for the final pay check of soldier Isadore Joseph Schwartz. This in itself was something of a landmark, as all previous requests for such documentation from both Norma and myself had been for a number of different Joseph Schwartzes. Hopefully when the pay check came back the signature on it would be an exact handwriting match to my mother's correspondence from Isadore.

After 34 years of disappointments, information about my father was now coming through at quite a pace, and this all had an air of unreality about it. But whatever my doubts might be, they clearly did not hold water over in Ann Arbor. LeAnn sent through a congratulatory email saying that she had called in to a supermarket en route to home in order to buy something British to celebrate with. Unfortunately only Weetabix and Marmite were available! A glass of wine would have to be a substitute, albeit a very suitable one.

The air of unreality was soon to recede, as another email from LeAnn soon came through. She had looked on the web for the name Marian Garfinkel at the location of Philadelphia. She then had found the website of an Iyengar Yoga specialist matching that name and residing in Philadelphia. The message from LeAnn finished with the words, "This could be your aunt".

I clicked on the link, and a page with a picture of a Dr Marian Garfinkel appeared. I stared long and hard at the smiling, youthful picture and compared it with a picture of myself aged 21. I found a definite likeness. Yet surely this could be just fantasy? In any event the time in Philadelphia was in the small hours, so I would have to wait for a more suitable moment to call her and find out.

Saturday February 7th 2010 was going to be a very important day for me as a supporter of my favourite football team, Swansea City. They had an important home fixture to play and kick-off time had been brought forward by two hours to 1 pm so as not to overlap with another major sports fixture in

South Wales. I remember that after a dreary winter it was a beautiful sunlit afternoon, which matched an excellent performance by my team, resulting in a 2-0 victory. I drove home in good spirits, remembering that there were two transatlantic phone calls I had to make. I intended to call both Marian Garfinkel and the Altoona Historical Society, who would be in session at Altoona Library all day Saturday.

So which one to make first? As it seemed highly unlikely that Marian could be my aunt it would, I thought, be a good idea to get that call over and done with first. Then I would have plenty of time to contact the society.

I dialled the Philadelphia number, and immediately a voice replied, "Marian Garfinkel".

"Hello, my name is Norman Spencer and I'm calling from the United Kingdom about a former friend of my family during the time of World War Two" I began. "He was called Isadore Joseph Schwartz. I wonder if you know of him, or are by any chance related to him?"

The reply came back immediately.

"Yes, he was my brother, Your family knew him during the war?"

I tried hard not to lapse into a stunned silence. So many phone calls asking about a Joseph Schwartz had been met with a negative response, and now it seemed I had hit the jackpot. So I had to improvise quickly and think of something to say. I went on to say that Isadore had been very highly thought of. Unfortunately we had lost touch over the years, but we had always wondered what had happened to him. In essence this was the truth, but not necessarily in the right order.

"Yes, he was my brother," said Marian. "I am looking at his army photograph right now. He's standing in front of his plane in Italy."

This was absolutely stunning!

I had to try and keep this exchange going for as long as possible. The conversation with the woman who was now definitely my long-lost aunt continued at a brisk pace for the next forty-five minutes. She seemed fascinated by my accent, and she appeared a very knowledgeable person. I have to admit that it was quite a strain keeping up the pretence while endeavouring to try and extract some information about my father.

My enquiry as to the reason why he had passed away at a relatively early age was gently side-stepped, and the topic moved onto various philosophies and religions and, inevitably, the weather. Apparently Philadelphia was snowbound at this time. One thing I did learn during this marathon conversation was that my father was known in the family as "Yossie".

Requesting my newly-discovered aunt's address, I promised to write to her enclosing some more information about myself, including a photograph. I concluded with the words "I think you will find the letter and photographs interesting". This was something of an understatement, but I was more concerned about the reaction to the forthcoming letter. I knew of several instances involving "GI babies" when someone had been able to prove their father's identity beyond reasonable doubt, only to be met with rejection and denial.

I finished the call by thanking her for listening. Marian, for her part, said that she would be phoning her sister in California to tell her all about a conversation with someone from the United Kingdom whose family knew their brother.

Replacing the receiver, I heard the first few words of our conversation repeating over and over in my head: "He was my brother". The significance of her words now began to strike home. I had actually spoken to a transatlantic relative for the very first time. It had been a pleasant, if slightly surreal experience, and one which would remain with me for a very long time.

There was now little point in calling the Historical Society. On the other hand I had to contact William Kibler in order to thank him but at the same time put him off the trail - at least for the time being. At this stage an article in the *Altoona Mirror* about Isadore Schwartz's illegitimate son could still undo everything I had worked to achieve.

I called William and, without revealing exactly where and with who, told him that I had established contact with one of the Schwartz family, so there would be no need for him to call round the Altoona neighbourhood.

The truth is elusive; it can slip through your fingers like water. I now told myself that I had done all I could to ensure that this did not happen to me. I felt that at this vital stage of my search a little more patience and a carefully-woven strategy would be the key to attaining further knowledge about the missing half of my identity.

A few hours later I began to ask myself some important questions. Did my aunt know about my existence anyway, and perhaps my phone call was not really a surprise? If not, then surely my father must had told someone that he had a son. If so, who?

Then came the realisation, however blindingly obvious it might be. He had long since passed away, and I would never be able to ask him these and other questions. I would never share life's experiences with him and express my anger at his apparent failure to return to England as he had promised.

Over and over again I wondered - why did he die so young? It just did not seem fair for everyone concerned, not for my mother, not for me, not for his family in the U. S.

Now there was the task of writing to my newly-discovered aunt, and a lot of thought had to be engaged in this task. I had to prepare a letter which would gently but informatively reveal exactly who I was, while simultaneously being not only plausible but also impressive. No easy task. Several drafts would have to be prepared before the finished article was despatched with both a hope and a prayer.

CHAPTER TWELVE

CONTACT

My letter to Marian Garfinkel had to be plausible and sincere, and it had to have the desired impact. When it comes to making a first impression you only get one chance, and this was mine. I began to draft a suitable text which would not only explain the circumstances which had led me to this life-changing discovery but underline the emotional need for every person on this earth to have some knowledge of their parents' character and background.

I needed to make it clear to Marian that no form of financial gain was being sought in any shape or form, not now or in the future. This had been the theme of all my correspondence with prospective Schwartzes in the past. Therefore it would be prudent to mention my own financial security - albeit modest - while at the same time emphasising my willingness to answer all relevant questions.

Perfection is not always achievable, but I set about trying to make this item of correspondence as near to perfect as possible. In order to achieve this I consulted the wise heads of both Professor David Jackson and LeAnn Fields. Their suggestions and ideas seemed to run more or less parallel with my own and so, after some three drafts, the letter was ready for printing and despatch.

My letter fell into two distinct parts. In the first I provided my life history in a redacted form. Then I went on to suggest that before reading the second part it might be wise for Marian to make sure that she was sitting down. In the second section I briefly sketched the key stages in my search. I ended the letter by stating that I believed I was indeed the biological son of former USAAF soldier Isadore Joseph Schwartz from Altoona PA.

Of course, I could have gone on fine-tuning my draft indefinitely, but had I done so there was the real prospect that the original sincerity and character of my message would have been lost. A stilted, formal letter was definitely not wanted.

I printed out the final version, which came to just over two A4 pages. I was satisfied with my efforts. I selected suitable photos of my mother and me illustrating the various stages of our respective lives. These I sealed in a smaller envelope, which I placed inside the mailing one. I wrote on the small envelope "please read my letter before opening". This way the material would be presented in a logical order.

The moment had now arrived when the letter and pictures were ready to be mailed.

On a misty, mild February morning I walked the two thirds of a mile to Caerphilly Post Office carrying the precious letter. As I waited my turn in the seemingly slow-moving queue I felt my stomach starting to react to what was obvious inner tension. What if the letter got mislaid? What if Marian refused to believe my story? What if she put off responding for ever and a day? What if…?

Before I had got to the 99th "What if" it was my turn to be served at the counter. I opted for the mail-delivery service which electronically tracks every stage in the transit of the letter and has to be signed for at its destination address. Then I made my way home, finally feeling a sense of relief.

That feeling was however destined to be but a transient one. I felt the need to read through my final version, imagining that I was reading it for the very first time. I started my PC. The letter came up and then I began to have a sinking feeling, the kind of feeling you get when an unintended oversight can have potentially disastrous consequences.

Everything I had compiled and printed was as immaculate as I could have made it – except for one vital item of information. At the top of the first page I had listed my home telephone number. In error I had then provided the international dialling code for calls from the UK to Germany!

It would create great confusion if Marian, upon receiving the letter, decided to call me only to find herself having "number unobtainable" coming back via a digital voice. Even worse would be some bewildered German wondering why on earth this American lady was calling.

Thinking on my feet I hotfooted it back to town. I purchased a Caerphilly postcard, on which I inscribed my correct dialling code and a brief note of apology. I placed it in the outgoing mailbox feeling confident that I had retrieved my rather basic error and that from now on, all would be well.

The next day I decided to make a visit to the town library and check out any books that might contain information about the United States forces in World War II. It wasn't an entirely unproductive visit, as I found an interesting publication about the USAAF 9th Air Force which had lavish illustrations and descriptions of the many different divisions that had served in the UK. Disappointingly, there did not seem to be any publications about the 8th Air Force (I had always believed that my father served in the 8th) but never mind. Only later would I discover that this book contained information which was far more valuable in terms of my search than I could have imagined.

As I walked along in the pale February sunshine, many different thoughts drifted through my mind regarding the letter I had sent. It was now on its way "Stateside" – maybe it was already airborne, maybe it was still in South Wales, or maybe it had already become one of the many items of correspondence sometimes mislaid by the Royal Mail!

When I got home, the morning mail had arrived. Among the items was a letter from home from Norma-Jean. She had forwarded the latest communication from the NPRC, who had responded to the request for the final pay check of Isadore J. Schwartz. As the USAAF final pay check records had not been stored in the same location as the full military records, they had escaped the disastrous 1973 St Louis fire. Three pages had been sent, listing other servicemen whose details had been appropriately blanked out.

On the third page opposite my father's typed name was a hurriedly written signature – Isadore J. Schwartz. There was confirmation that he had received the $300 mustering-out payment awarded only to those servicemen who had served overseas. The signature appeared to match the handwriting in the fading letters sent to my mother. I could not be 100% sure of this, and for days afterwards would check again and again by holding the signature alongside the letters. I wanted every shadow of doubt to be removed.

A week went by, and it seemed like a month. Every subsequent day seemed like an eternity as I waited for a response from Marian. At last the mail tracking system indicated that the precious letter had arrived in the United States and was awaiting further despatch to its final destination in Philadelphia.

What kind of discussion would take place all those thousands of miles away? What thoughts would go through people's minds? I could only speculate on this, and hope that they were mainly positive ones and would initiate a favourable response. There had been past instances when TRACE members had submitted irrevocable evidence of their father's identity, only to be rejected out of hand.

I wondered if Marian would tell me about any prospective half-sisters and brothers, what their facial appearance might be, their personalities and what relationship they had had with their father.

Then, as if to break the growing tension, the Caerphilly library called me. The two books I had ordered had come in and were ready for collection.

"Two books? But I haven't ordered two books. What are they about, please?"

Apparently they were both novels. I never read novels and would never have ordered any. But my curiosity got the better of me (as usual), and I made my way to the library to inspect the phantom order.

The publications were both by the same author. One was about a man who became very successful, leaving behind the hometown girl he had planned to marry and instead marrying the daughter of the senior partner of the firm he worked for. The second book was about a young lady who gets to go to University, only to find out that that her father was not the man she thought was so wonderful but is instead a master of deception.

Whether this was pure coincidence or something deeper I will probably never know, but I do know that I read both these publications, albeit quickly, and gained a little more understanding of the possible future problems I could be confronted with.

The tension was mounting now with every single day that passed, and to counteract this I had to keep reminding myself how much further forward I had come compared to this time last year, or indeed just a few weeks ago.

The tracking system still refused to confirm arrival at the mailing destination, and my concern was that it had got lost. Then suddenly, as if out of the blue, the telephone rang. I picked it up. Marian Garfinkel was on the end of the line.

"Norman, thank you very much for sending me the nice postcard of Caerphilly," she said. "Now I am able to call you when it is convenient for me".

"Did you receive my letter, Marian?"

"No - you have sent a letter as well?"

Now I found myself in an unplanned and somewhat tricky situation - the postcard had overtaken the letter in their respective transatlantic journeys!

For the next 45 minutes an interesting conversation ensued about yoga, philosophy, the modern world, my affinity with Native American spirituality and every conceivable topic under the sun - except the one I really had in mind. I had to exercise real personal discipline in order to conceal my true identity. To reveal this at this stage would surely ruin the impact and possibility of a response to my carefully crafted item of correspondence.

Halfway through this protracted exchange, Marian suddenly posed a question to me: "Are you Jewish?" I had to give a politician's response by evading a direct answer to the question and skilfully changing the subject. Even hinting at the possibility that there might be some Jewish lineage (as yet unproven at this time) in my family tree could, to use a Hollywood phrase, have blown my cover, and sent Marian running.

I used the tried and tested British way of getting out of an awkward situation. "We are all inter-related in some way," I said. "How is the weather in Philadelphia today?" The weather – the standard diversion when everything around you is falling down!

Eventually our conversation came to a natural ending. It had been a slightly nerve-racking but nonetheless pleasurable experience, which had been prolonged by Marian's fascination with my accent.

On Saturday February 27th the tracking system provided the information that I had been waiting for. My letter had been delivered and signed for at Marian Garfinkel's Philadelphia address.

That same evening a production of the musical *Carousel* was being performed at a small out-of-town theatre in Cardiff. I decided to obtain a ticket to attend. Carousel is probably the only Hollywood-style musical that really appeals to me, and not without good reason. It tells the story of a young and wayward father who gets into a lot of trouble. He is killed in an unsavoury incident and then finds himself up in heaven, working as a star-polisher. The theme continues when the chief star keeper informs him that there is an allowance for everyone to have the opportunity to return back down to the earth, but for only 24 hours. During that time the person concerned will be given every opportunity within the rules to put right all the wrongs that they had committed during their lifetime there. The parallel with my father's life is not strictly accurate, but near enough to have some relevance to me.

The show was really good, although my concentration wandered at times as my thoughts drifted to what might be happening far across the Atlantic. Would the final outcome of years of searching with all the energy expended and blind alleys encountered have been worth it?

I did not have to wait too long. The following day I received the vital phone call. The unmistakable voice of Marian came through with the words:

"Oh Norman, what can I say about all this? It is a remarkable discovery and I know that my sister in California will be very pleased to know about it."

It seemed that no one had been aware of my existence far away in the United Kingdom. At last the connection I had yearned for had finally come to pass. It provided the realisation that some kind of acceptance had finally been forged with members of my father's family.

Because of the time difference, it would be a few hours before Marian would be able to contact her sister, Ruth Johns. The conversation eventually ended with an assurance that I would be hearing from that neck of the woods very shortly.

Sure enough, the very next evening the phone rang, and I picked it up to hear: "Norman, this is Ruth speaking. I am your aunt and you - you are my new nephew".

Truly astonishing, and at the same time heartwarming. I was actually speaking to a second person who was directly related to my father, and to me. When Marian had called to inform her of my existence, the conversation had begun with the words, "Are you sitting or standing? Sit down – you won't believe this."

Marian had warned me that Ruth was not in the best of health. I felt it was important to take great care not to sound like some kind of interrogator, although there were a thousand questions to which I sought answers.

During this initial conversation Ruth, who was by now my "Aunt Ruth", revealed several snippets of information with very little prompting by myself. She confirmed what Marian had told me, that my father had been actively involved in the D-Day military operations.

For many years my admiration for the men who had taken part in that apparently suicidal exercise had been growing. From the many movies and documentaries to the surviving blurred Robert Capra images, I had been in total awe of the bravery and sacrifice shown on that momentous day for Europe and the free world. Now I was being told that my father had played a part in it. I felt a real sense of pride knowing this.

Knowing my aunt was in poor health, I did not pester her with questions. I simply listened to what she had to say about my father and other members of the family. It turned out that Isadore, who was known in the family as Yossie, was a "sweet person" who was liked by everyone who knew him.

Eventually the conversation came to a natural end. "I hope we keep in touch," said Aunt Ruth. Keep in touch? For me, after 34 years of fruitless searching, there was no possibility of anything other than keeping in touch!

The following few weeks continued on this theme. Every time we talked I learned a little more about my long-lost family far across the ocean. Aunt Ruth spoke of several pictures of my father and of a wartime 78 rpm recording he had made at an army training establishment. She promised to send them when they had been sorted. I could not wait to see the pictures and hear the recording. To me they meant everything, and would be some form of compensation for the years of having only a single sepia wartime photograph to look at, together with some items of wartime correspondence which by now were starting to disintegrate.

In April an email from Ruth's son, Scott, arrived. Tentatively welcoming me to the family, he went on to give some recollections of my "apparent father" which were of a positive nature. He was described as a "kindly and exuberant". Scott explained that he would have been around seven years old at the time of his last encounter so these were only fleeting impressions.

Equally relevant was the praise from Scott's father Theron. According to him all the other family members had thought very highly of my father, valued his character, and had especially appreciated his thoughtfulness.

Scott had attached to his email a photograph of my father aged thirteen, when he would have attended his Bar Mitzvah. When I compared the image with one of myself at a similar age it left little doubt that I was indeed this man's son.

At the end of the email Scott provided me with the exact location of my father's grave at the Eden Memorial Park in the San Fernando Valley. I looked at this last piece of information over and over again and came to the inevitable conclusion. I had to go and see for myself his final resting place, and I had to do it soon.

Now I had to wrestle with how to approach this proposed visit and how to achieve maximum results from a minimum itinerary. The weeks were racing by and there was still no sign of the promised photographs and the 78 rpm record. There seemed no urgency or motivation for them to be sent. In fairness to my aunt, it appeared that she was having great difficulty in organising the necessary items and secure packaging. She was unwell, and it would be unfair to keep on pressing the issue.

Telephone conversations between California, Philadelphia and Caerphilly were now taking place on a frequent basis. Each time I learned a little more about the new part of my family and the father I had never known.

Marian had indicated earlier that she intended to be in the United Kingdom on June 6th (The anniversary of D-Day, so a very significant date in European history) and that I could meet her in London around that time. I eagerly anticipated meeting her, and made provisional plans to bring her to Caerphilly and give a grand tour of my beautiful adopted homeland. Regrettably this did not happen, as due to other commitments, Marian had to cancel her trip. Once again my desire to establish contact and rapport with my father's family had been thrown into disarray.

Telephone conversations are informing and sometimes uplifting, but they have their limitations. There is no substitute for a face-to-face meeting.

I still kept wondering about the results of my search and their consequences. What had happened to the mysterious St Louis "Mary" and her child? Why did my father decide to effectively airbrush me out of his life in a typewritten letter from that city? What had caused him to abandon his university studies? Had he ever told anyone about his English wartime romance and the son that arrived as a result of it? And most of all, how did he come to die so young ?

There is a song by Johnny Nash with a line that goes, "There are more questions than answers". Indeed there are, and if I was going to get any more answers there was only one obvious course of action. I had to go to California.

CHAPTER THIRTEEN

FAMILY REUNION

Over the next few weeks, information by phone from my two aunts flowed freely across the Atlantic, though it wasn't really direct information about my father. My two new relatives were more focused on relaying their own life stories, which I regarded as an added bonus.

Slowly but surely it was becoming possible to construct a picture of the missing half of my identity. At the same time, however, all this new information was throwing up other questions which needed to be answered.

From now on there was no looking back. One slight exception was a momentary flashback to an image I had carried around with me for some 45 years. During my time working as an apprentice electrician in Suffolk, I had on several occasions accompanied the electrician to whom I was assigned to work at two local airfields, the USAAF bases at Woodbridge and Bentwaters.

To visit these places was a fascinating experience. To me they were mirror images of what I imagined life in America was like. When we entered one of the bases, my 17-year-old eyes would be starstruck. There were shops and workshops, highways and dormitories, all laid out in the style of the Hollywood movies screened in local cinemas. The uniformed US servicemen going about their daily tasks made for a supporting cast. It all had a surreal feel about it. Had John Wayne, Kirk Douglas, Audie Murphy etc suddenly appeared from one of the many US-style buildings there, it would have come as no great surprise.

One of the electricians, who was nicknamed Dixie Dean, was equally fascinated by the bases. The tall, sometimes fiery but always diligent Dixie - his mother was Spanish - had been promoted from apprentice to electrician at the tender age of 19. He may not have been a technical genius, but he had certainly set the bar high for other apprentices in terms of commitment. His achievement was something to strive for.

On one occasion I accompanied Dixie to undertake a task at the base's ammunition compound. His fascination had much to do with the fact that we had an armed soldier to escort and oversee us during our work at the compound.

"Did you see the shooter that soldier was carrying?" he excitedly asked me. In truth I had paid little attention to any weaponry. Instead I had been fascinated by the floors of the dormitories with their mirror-like cleanliness, by the various large American cars around the base and by the soldiers wearing baseball caps. Somehow all these things struck a chord with me.

May 13th 2010, the day of my departure, finally arrived. There is always a certain amount of anxiety involved when you are going on a journey, and this journey was not only going to be long but adventurous and possibly life-changing. Various events conspired to produce butterflies in my stomach. The gigantic cloud of ash caused by the eruption of an Icelandic volcano threw domestic and international flights into complete chaos. Flights were either cancelled completely or considerably delayed. My impending trip was now completely in the lap of the gods.

The thought was also crossing my mind that I had no idea whatsoever what my newly-found relatives actually looked like. I had sent several pictures of myself, but nothing had come back in return. Added to this was a minor communication problem with Ruth's husband, Theron. On a couple of occasions when I telephoned, and he had answered, he appeared to have some difficulty understanding what I was saying. Was it my accent or the speed with which I talked that caused the problem? Or was it perhaps that he didn't really want to communicate?

In short, I was about to embark on a journey where my comfort zone would be left far behind. The words of the late Pamela Winfield constantly came to mind - "have no regrets". This strengthened my desire to succeed.

My cousin in California, Scott Johns, emailed to say that when I arrived at Oceanside Railroad Station Theron would be there to assist in transportation to my hotel in Carlsbad. After receiving this message I felt a little easier about my journey.

It was a cool, calm spring morning when my friend John Andrews arrived at my house to take me by car to Cardiff. There I would catch the train en route for London's Heathrow Airport. As the train pulled out of Cardiff station, I felt a sense of relief and anticipation that at long last my mission was under way. The fields and meadows outside my carriage window were already lighting up with the early morning sun, and a soft mist clung to the dips and hollows in the landscape. Everything looked truly beautiful. For a few minutes an aura of calm had entered my world.

The check-in, boarding and take-off were smooth and efficient. The following eleven hours passed without event, save for a moment when the flight captain said, "Look out of the window on your forward right, where you can observe the remains of the volcanic ash cloud which has caused chaos in transatlantic airline schedules recently".

Los Angeles International Airport had last been graced with my presence some thirty years previously when I had flown back to the UK following a three-week coast-to-coast camping trek. Back then I had not envisaged ever returning to America, let alone on such an important mission.

Having cleared customs and collected my baggage, I made my way outside to the concourse. My anticipated shuttle lift to the local Travelodge was proving somewhat problematical. There was a myriad of different shuttle buses arriving to unload and pick up their respective clients, but there did not appear to be one relating to my particular hotel and I was getting impatient and anxious and feeling more than a little bit tired.

All around me there was activity with people alighting, disembarking and pacing up and down. One particular individual caught my attention, an overweight, middle-aged man dressed in smart casual clothing complete with the regulatory sunglasses. He appeared to be looking into the near distance without ever actually locating the vehicle or person he sought. What, I asked myself, was he doing on the terminal concourse?

By the time I had waited for over an hour, my patience was at breaking point. Luckily the driver of a rival company offered me a lift. As I closed the door of the mini-bus I glanced outside. The mysterious man had disappeared.

In no time at all I was being dropped off at my hotel. Thanking my helpful driver, and making sure that he was suitably tipped, I made my way to the reception area. At the desk I learned that the hotel shuttle did not operate in the mid-afternoon!

Having checked in, I made my way through the sprawling

complex to my room. I prepared for bed and after a very few minutes, I felt myself drifting away. Soon I was fast asleep, oblivious to the frequent noises of landing aircraft.

I think it must have been some time in the early hours when I awoke, noticing that at the far side of my room a light was flashing. This was not particularly disconcerting as no sound accompanied it. Before long I once again lapsed into a state of unconsciousness.

The following morning I woke up before my alarm rang, went downstairs to the breakfast bar and came back to collect my belongings ready for the trip to Los Angeles Union Station. Just before leaving my room for the last time, a thought suddenly struck me: what had the flashing light been? It dawned on me that the light must have been from the phone in my room. An LED was still flashing opposite a button marked "messages". I picked up the receiver and pressed the button.

"Norman, this is Ruth speaking" it said. "Welcome to the United States, I hope you had a good journey. Call me as soon as you can please. Thank you".

This was indeed an unexpected greeting, and much appreciated. I would have to try to return the call when I arrived at Union Station. It was a nice feeling to have my arrival recognised by someone who only a few weeks before had had no knowledge of my existence.

I collected my baggage together, checked out and took the hotel shuttle back to the airport. From the concourse I caught the Flyaway bus to Union Station. Upon arriving I enlisted the use of a receptionist's mobile phone to contact my Aunt Ruth (all public telephones were inoperable), thanking her for the pleasant greeting and confirming my estimated time of arrival at Oceanside railroad station.

Union Station itself was a striking building with art deco design and the ambience of a bygone age when travel was more gentle and sophisticated. The Surfliner southbound double-decker train I boarded was impressive and elegant. It slowly wound its way out of Los Angeles through several goods yards and suburbs. Finally the Pacific Ocean came into view. Occasionally the train sounded its whistle, a long, echoing tone, as if it was breaking through one of the last frontiers of the old West.

Outside my window, an eagle-like bird circled in the sky. People were picking crops in the fields. By contrast the opposite window afforded a view of the ocean, which on this particular day looked somewhat grey and uninviting. The calming effect of the smooth ride and elevated view of the varying scenery was proving to be an interesting journey.

The time of my rendezvous with Theron and eventually Aunt Ruth was drawing ever closer. I had to remind myself that I had come here with zero expectations. Everything above that would be a bonus.

As the train arrived at Oceanside station I felt the hand of destiny reaching out to touch my shoulder. I alighted quickly to see a lone figure awaited me by the ticket office. It was Ruth's husband Theron, and he greeted me in a quiet, unfamiliar accent.

As we drove the few miles along the coast to Carlsbad, Theron gave me a brief outline of the local landmarks and attractions. By now I had determined that his family originated from northern Florida and he had come to California many years before. This explained why he had not understood me on the phone. A Florida accent is delivered slowly, with precision. My South Walian lilt, though slight, must have sounded like something from another planet to Theron!

When we arrived at my hotel in Carlsbad, Theron left me to unpack and unwind and promised to call back one hour later to take me to meet Ruth at their house. This hour seemed endless, so it was with some relief that I eventually found myself at the home of my aunt. Neat and unpretentious, the house was one of many on a typical suburban private Californian estate. The neighbourhood appeared quiet and orderly.

"Ruth is just getting ready upstairs, so if you'd care to sit down she will be with you shortly" said Theron. Another wait, and my mind began to wander over the events of the past year or so. I must have been deep in thought, which was suddenly interrupted by a woman's voice saying "Norman!" There standing in the doorway, immaculately dressed, was a slightly-built elderly lady, with distinctive Jewish features and a kindly smile.

For a few seconds, time seemed to stand still. I looked at this figure standing a few feet away from me and knew that this was the defining moment in the search for my American heritage. I realised that my heritage was not so much American as Jewish. In many ways this fact had always been hovering in the background, and now it had come to the fore.

I stood up and went over to greet this lady, my aunt. It was like the scene in a mystery movie where the final twist in the tale is at last revealed.

"Norman, how are you?" she said. "It's wonderful to see you. Come and sit down and tell me about your trip."

From our phone conversations I had somehow formed a picture of Ruth as being much larger in physique than the lady now sitting opposite me. It may sound simplistic, but what I was finding really difficult was the realisation that I was now actually face to face with my father's sister. My father's sister! This was someone he had grown up with, with whom he'd lived under the same roof, in the same time. He would probably have told her of his ambitions and fears. The knowledge that she had been with my father during his final hours made her even more special.

I knew that in recent years Aunt Ruth's health had been declining, and because of this I had promised Scott that I would not cause his mother any stress. So I just sat and listened carefully to what she was saying, while holding myself ready to answer any questions. I had to avoid the temptation to take on the guise of an interrogator. I had, after all, come to California to learn all I could about my father in the hope of understanding something of his character and the reasoning behind certain difficult decisions he had taken.

As the day ticked by, the details of my father's life story were slowly but surely being revealed to me. It had been a life of great adventure, tempered with disappointments, but not without some achievements.

"He was still looking for his niche in life when he died," said Ruth. My aunt's observation pulled at my heartstrings. I had not experienced this emotion about my father before.

The story of my aunt's life was in itself interesting and involved that well-known mecca for glamour and intrigue - Hollywood. She had worked there at the Paramount Pictures studios. I was told of different incidents involving Liberace, Alfred Hitchcock, Howard da Silva, George Sanders and a one-time possible romance with the actor Jeff Chandler, which had fizzled out before it had started.

Towards the end of the day one particular family recollection did prove to be of significance to me. It was about a time when my father had visited them. He had taken Scott in his arms and whirled him round the room. Young Scott did not react too kindly to this boisterous act of affection and used to cry out, "Put me down! Put me down! "

I wondered what had been going through my father's mind at this time. Had he simply been going through the motions of being the favourite uncle, or was he re-enacting what he wished he could have done with his own son? I will never know, but my aunt's innocent recollection was burning me up inside.

Aunt Marian had sent Ruth the copy of the letter my father had seemingly sent from St Louis to my mother. I knew she must have read it, and gently asked her how much, if anything, she had previously known about the story in the letter. After a few seconds she replied to say that she had never known anything about my father being in St Louis, let alone marrying anyone from there! It seemed that my father's story of marrying a pregnant wife called Mary and emigrating to South America was a complete fabrication.

In some respects this revelation did not come as a total surprise. Some of the people who had helped me in my search in the past had expressed scepticism about the story. They had suspected a hidden agenda.

I now felt there was a missing period in my father's post-war activities and this was confirmed when Theron, who had been patiently listening in on our conversation, interjected: "Yossie – he came out to California sometime in the fall of 1947. He found a job working for what I think was a power and water company – I believe he was doing some kind of testing and inspection for them. For a short while he worked on a trial probationary basis. Apparently they were very pleased with the quality of his work. But when they offered him the position permanently he failed the medical examination and lost the job – he was deeply disappointed about that. Then we lost contact with him for a while. I think he drifted back out east somewhere".

More intrigue, more unanswered questions.

It's only natural that one always want to think the best of one's parents. It would be true to say that in relation to the South America story, I had developed a blind spot. I had hoped against hope that at least some part of the story my father told my mother was true, and that eventually I would be meet up with my half siblings. This news left me with a deep sense of disappointment, especially on my mother's behalf, that it was all a fabrication. To her the St Louis story must have seemed an honourable explanation for my father's failure to return to England after the war ended.

Now I was told that my father had later married someone by the name of Shirley. She had been married before, and had a daughter called Beth. They had been married a mere five and a half years when my father died, and Shirley and Beth had then disappeared. I asked how it was possible for them to just simply vanish. "We don't know where they went to after the funeral and we don't want to know" was the reply given.

I decided to wait until the next day to pursue this further, as my aunt was becoming weary. But something else was kicking into my psyche – the realisation that I must have been my father's only child. How must that have felt to him when, as sure as night follows day, he must have witnessed other families with children, sons in particular, and wondered at what might have been or, more pertinently, what should have been?

There would be one more relevant event on this first day at my aunt's house. I was to meet her son, Scott Johns, who effectively was my first cousin. Scott had telephoned his mother earlier in the day to say that he and all his family were ill as they were suffering from a virus and might have to cancel a planned get-together on the coming Sunday evening. I was therefore surprised when, shortly before I was about to leave for my hotel, a call came through for my aunt. It was Scott - he was on his way over and would be there in a few minutes.

A 4x4 vehicle drove up and stopped outside, and cousin Scott emerged from it. We gathered outside to greet him, Ruth, Theron and myself, and by this time dusk had fallen. In the gloom I could just about make out a slight figure, who began by greeting his parents in a distinctive Californian accent.

"Hello, it's nice to meet you" I said, holding out my hand to greet him. Scott was reluctant to shake my hand, explaining that he did not want me to contract the unknown virus. I was having none of this. After all, I hadn't travelled 5000 miles only to miss the chance to shake hands for the first time with my cousin.

That done, Scott asked "So, what's on the itinerary?" I was slightly taken aback, and replied, "There's nothing in particular on the itinerary, I've simply come here to learn". It seemed a strange question to ask me. It was as if I was some kind of tourist.

I had hoped that his first impression of me was a good one, as you only get one chance to make a first impression. Some time later I managed to form an understanding of cousin Scott's initially slightly reluctant nature. In fairness, when you are suddenly informed at the age of 50 that you have a living relative in the United Kingdom, it takes a little while to absorb it, let alone believe it. For 34 years I had been searching for my father and his relatives. Scott had known about me for less than three months. It does not follow that you should be automatically enthusiastic about such a meeting. After all, you cannot feel the same need to be accepted.

As I relaxed in my hotel room that night, my thoughts drifted to a spring morning in Paris a few years before. The sun was shining gently through the trees alongside the River Seine as I approached the Palais de Chaillot, a well-known Parisian landmark and the site of two very good museums. Outside the sculptured buildings a band was playing a medley of wartime favourites. Suddenly I heard the strains of "Somewhere beyond the sea" and my mind turned to my American father. Was he indeed "beyond the sea" with his wife Mary and the children who would be my half brothers and sisters? I had thought he must be, whether it be in North or South America, and that one day I would find him and maybe bring a happy ending to all this longing to know about my true identity. Now in the solitude of my hotel room I knew that this illusion had gone forever, and totally different images were entering my subconscious.

I had three days left to try and get to the truth, three days to establish some concrete facts. Above all I had to see if Aunt Ruth had any photographs of my father and the life he had led. Tomorrow could not come quick enough.

The following day was more or less a repeat of the previous one. Theron graciously collected me from the hotel and took me to their home for breakfast. My aunt continued on the same theme, with additional stories of other relatives and the revelation that some of those relatives on her mother's side (my grandmother) had perished in the holocaust.

She began with the line "I have relatives in..." and then paused for a second. Then she said to me, "of course, they are your relatives too". A brief description of names and locations of other family members in the United States, Europe and Israel followed. Although I did not grasp every detail, it was reassuring at least to have this acknowledgment of my blood association with the Schwartz family.

Her account of my father's final hours made a deep impression on me. She gave vague details of a matrimonial dispute which had resulted in my father having to drive himself to the local hospital in order to obtain medical care and treatment. After entering the hospital he never came out of it alive, and my aunt had been there with him during his final hours.

The speed of his demise had led to a frantic scramble to obtain a suitable casket. As the Jewish religion requires burial before sundown the following day, my aunt had to move very quickly to ensure this procedure was followed.

During the second day at my aunt's house I noticed a photo album underneath the coffee table and asked whether I could look at it. "Of course you can," she said.

I began to go through the pages. Inside there were many pictures of Aunt Ruth's adventures around the world. Also, and this really was a discovery, I came across pictures of my grandparents enjoying their 50th wedding anniversary celebration in Los Angeles in 1965. The unmistakable image of my father appeared in these celebratory images, and I found myself staring at these for minutes on end. Until this moment the only photograph I had seen was the wartime uniformed one which my mother had kept all those years, and the recently emailed picture taken of him at his Bar Mitzvah. Using my camera I quickly recorded these unexpected bonuses.

I wondered if there were any more photographs of him, and gently inquired of my aunt as to their possible whereabouts. I was told they were "somewhere upstairs" and that she would look for them later.

A story was then related to me concerning a wartime escapade in Paris. My father had been lodging at a château within the city and had somehow managed to acquire a live chicken. Holding it tightly, he had then made the journey to his lodgings using the Paris Metro. During the journey he had been offered payment for the chicken by several other passengers on the Metro. By all accounts my father had resisted the temptation to sell his potential meal. The enthusiasm of the potential purchasers had in turn illustrated how desperate the civilian food supply had become in that city. Apparently when the chicken finally reached its intended destination, there was amazement at how the owners of the château had worked wonders to make virtually all the chicken edible! My aunt found this story very amusing.

This story made me remember the many excursions I had undertaken around the Paris Metro system. It formed in my mind an image of a USAAF serviceman on a chaotic, comedic Parisian journey.

The next day, a Sunday, we were due to go for dinner to cousin Scott's house in the nearby coastal beach city of Encinitas. Before that I once again listened to some more of my aunt's life stories. I particularly enjoyed the ones relating to her time working at the Hollywood studios of Paramount Pictures. Here was a woman who had led a remarkably active life, coupled together with a determination to achieve a high academic status in society.

When we arrived at Scott's house, which stood in an elevated position in a pleasant neighbourhood, I wondered what the reaction might be to the visit of a cousin who, until a few months' ago, to all intents and purposes, never existed. I need not have worried. In a brief few minutes the introduction to wife Paula, sons Adam and Joshua and Jet the dog were complete.

It is not my normal style to talk about myself to anyone. On this occasion it was necessary, however, and I gave a brief outline of my life, my search for my father and how it had all come to fruition.

A pleasant meal prepared by Paula followed, and there was an exchange of pleasantries with Adam and Joshua. Here once again I had to pinch myself with the realisation that these two young men were indeed, my relatives.

As we left I took care to mention that many members of the Transatlantic Children's Enterprise had applied for, and been granted, citizenship of the United States. I had set this objective in my mind some time before and hoped that Scott and Ruth would be willing to assist me in the future when it came to legally confirming my family identity to the relevant state authorities in London and Washington. Scott assured me that when the time came for my application to be presented he would assist in providing the necessary confirmation of their acceptance of my identity. Theron also made it known to me that he thought I had a genuine entitlement to citizenship. This was music to my ears.

Monday was my final day in Carlsbad, and the objective was to find, view and copy the photographs of my father. This was, of course, dependent on my aunt being able to locate them. She had not felt well enough to look for them the previous day, so this would be my last opportunity.

Shortly after breakfast I made my request for her to find the pictures. My aunt took some persuading, as she again felt unwell, rather than unwilling. Eventually we made our way to the room upstairs, where archives of past photography were stored. The minutes ticked by as the vast number of pictures were checked through. One by one she eliminated them as not being what we were looking for. I was beginning to despair. In a few hours I would be boarding the train back to Los Angeles.

The piles of irrelevant photographs were by now stacking up. Then I suddenly looked over towards the desk on my left and there, in a neat group, were a number of unsorted pictures. I leant over and inspected the contents. Almost without exception they contained images of my father, right from childhood to later life. There were even a few colour prints, and I felt enormous relief to finally have these precious items in my possession. Naturally I asked permission to take the items home with me, and this was granted.

A strange thought entered my head. I had looked at the desk several times during the search that afternoon but had had no recollection of seeing the group of pictures. It was almost as though they had materialised out of nowhere. Aunt Ruth didn't understand how they had appeared either. "Where did they come from? They weren't there before," she said.

Downstairs I made another perusal through the pictures. One in particular had caught my eye. It was a picture of my father dressed in smart casual clothing wearing designer sunglasses. Call it coincidence if you like, but this image closely resembled the middle-aged man who had been pacing up and down the concourse at Los Angeles airport.

At last I had a good selection of precious pictures to take back home with me to Wales. That evening Aunt Marian called from her home in Philadelphia to wish me luck for my upcoming visit to Eden Memorial Cemetery. There I would pay my respects at my father's grave. She also told me that everyone wished for Ruth to enjoy better health and that I should emphasise that on my departure.

The following morning I did just that, telling my aunt that

I loved her and wanted her to get better and that I would return again some time in the future. At Oceanside Station I bade farewell and thank you to Theron and boarded the train. Soon I was enjoying a beer on the upstairs deck. As the train sped northwards I looked out at the striking view of the Pacific coastline. My time in Carlsbad had been a good experience.

The next day would see me in the San Fernando Valley at the Eden Memorial Park - the final resting place of my father, Isadore Joseph Schwartz.

CHAPTER FOURTEEN

LAST RESTING PLACE

My journey on board the Surfliner took me once again through the sprawling suburbs of Los Angeles and from there to the suburb of Glendale. I had chosen to stay there in order to gain quick access to San Fernando by train. One of Glendale's many claims to fame is that Hollywood actor John Wayne spent a lot of his early formative years there. I didn't exactly feel like John Wayne, but there was an element of exploring the "new frontier" about my visit.

Having checked into my hotel shortly after midday, I decided to explore the neighbourhood. I also needed to seek out some suitable gifts to take home to Wales. I headed to what seemed to be a proliferation of shops and cafés when the traffic lights on the adjacent road turned to red. Suddenly the dulcet tones of Frank Sinatra came wafting through the airways at a high level of decibels. I was more than a little surprised to hear the car stereo systems around me blaring out "New York, New York". Back home in Wales anyone playing this particular genre of music would be looked upon as very old-fashioned.

The waiting cars all moved off the instant the lights turned to green – and Frank sang on. For a brief moment I wondered if the single beer I'd drunk on the train had contained some magic ingredient. Then the penny dropped. Every street lamp post in this part of Glendale had a grille at its base containing a loudspeaker, and the lamp posts were broadcasting Sinatra's greatest hits.

Thinking that this really was some wild, wacky place, I continued round the corner to a large plaza. A notice declared "Welcome to the Americana at Brand". Shops, cinemas, fountains and a park were all rolled into one central square. It aptly fitted the phrase "Only in America".

A young man was demonstrating remote-controlled model robot cars, and he invited me to try my hand at controlling one of them. Controlling high-end electronic toys is not one of my life's ambitions, but on this occasion I thought it might help me unwind from the previous few days' experiences. I quickly came to the conclusion that my expertise in these matters was poor, so I handed the control module back to the demonstrator. Passing the time of day, I enquired where he was from (my assumption was Mexico or somewhere further south), and after a few guesses, he told me he had been born in Israel.

With my father being of American Jewish origin, my instinct was to engage in conversation further, which I did, and this was to give me an interesting insight into the modern way of Jewish thinking and culture. Niv Goren (this was the young man's name) had recently been serving in the Israeli Army, but was now back in the US, where he had become an American citizen. He was making a living working on this electronic toy stall in the "Americana". The conversation continued at length and I eventually told Niv what the purpose of my presence in Glendale was and how the following day I was going to a big and testing event in my life.

The next morning the temperature was already in the low

70s when I set off from my hotel and returned to Glendale railroad station, a walk of a mile and a half. I needed to walk rather than take a cab or bus to keep a clear head and a focus on the task ahead. A Bruce Springsteen song kept running through my mind, a song about a Vietnam veteran who, after horrific war experiences, comes back home to be feted as a hero: "You can call me Joe, buy me a drink and shake my hand". I ran through this line a few times as I walked along. It was early, and somehow I felt optimistic about the day ahead. I passed a schoolyard where some young students were raising the American flag prior to commencing classes. Their educational experience that day was going to be very different from mine.

At the railroad station, the timetable indicated that the next train to San Fernando was not due for another hour and a half. It seemed a good time to seek out some breakfast. Some locals directed me to a small café on a nearby industrial estate which proved to be just the ticket. Only a few people were using this café, but they were an interesting cross-section of local clientele.

One customer in particular caught my eye. he was sitting down with a large book in front of him and scanning it with a magnifying glass. Just as I was about to make my departure we made eye contact and I made a brief, polite enquiry as to what the text of the book contained. When the reply came back that it was the Bible, I felt a slight reticence, as any type of religious fanatic advocating their particular interpretation is anathema to me.

I sensed that this person was not an extremist and engaged further in conversation. Here was a man who had turned his life around through turning to religion, and studying the Bible at every opportunity was his hobby. I mentioned the fact that in an hour or so I hoped to locate my father's grave in a Jewish cemetery, and he revealed a pendant around his neck containing the star of David. It turned out that this was a keepsake from a Jewish friend, and that he always carried it with him in remembrance.

We parted on the best of terms, and I wondered how much of a coincidence that chance meeting was.

Boarding the local train, it was time once more to witness the vast, urban sprawl that is the Los Angeles area and muse on another bygone hit song, "Last Train to San Fernando". This was of course not the last train to San Fernando but one on a regular schedule, but soon it was pulling into San Fernando, just like the words in the song.

The rail journey was timed at approximately 25 minutes, and by way of distraction, a trio of people in the attire of office workers were conducting a very lively conversation. I could not catch all that was being said (the dialect was strong and the delivery rapid) but what I did pick up contained several humorous anecdotes about various politicians and show business stars. All this helped to lighten the serious business that lay ahead of me, and in today's ever-faster modern world, it was nice to see people going to work with smiles on their faces. Their good humour distracted me from the serious business which lay ahead.

San Fernando railroad station turned out to be little more than a short platform with a tiny bus-stop type waiting shelter. Disembarking, I bade farewell to my humorous travelling companions and consulted my map. It had always been my intention to walk the two miles from the railroad station to the cemetery. In a sense this was the culmination of my search and bound to have some symbolic significance. Already the temperature was soaring, but my preparations for this were coming into play. A sunhat, light clothing and water were the order of the day, though I did make a brief stop at a little shop to purchase a cold drink.

Someone behind me called out to me in a gruff voice and I turned to see an unshaven vagrant slumped on the grass verge clutching a bottle. It was like a scene from a Clint Eastwood Spaghetti Western.

My steps took me past a vast freeway overpass, at which point my calculations told me that the cemetery would be a less than half a mile ahead. Soon the boundary fence of the memorial park appeared on my right. I was getting very close now and feeling tense, but relieved that my map-reading abilities had not let me down.

Then at last the main gates came into view and, to my horror, they were locked and chained! Posted below the chains was a notice in large capital letters: "CEMETERY CLOSED IN OBSERVANCE OF SHAVOUT".

For a few minutes I stood in stunned disbelief. A few days earlier my aunt had explained the procedure to be observed when entering and leaving a Jewish cemetery. Men had to wear a yarmulke (skull-cap) as a sign of the humbling relationship between God and man. Aunt Ruth had provided me with one to wear at the cemetery. Also, when leaving the site of a grave you must wash your hands in the fountain provided. This is done to mark the departure from the surroundings of death and to signify a renewed attachment with life.

I had readily promised to carry out these instructions, come suitably equipped and now, after travelling some 5000 miles, was faced with this situation. For a few brief seconds I shook the handles of the gates in despair and frustration. There was no possibility of failure here – there could not be.

I contemplated climbing over the high fencing. This would be difficult but not impossible, though it would be a last resort. High above, the midday sun was shining down with a vengeance. The heat was becoming really oppressive. How was it that my aunt, who had been so particular about procedure, had not seen fit to warn me of this barring of access to the cemetery? Cousin Scott had kindly located the exact address of the row and plot that my father was located in, so how had he not also realised that my visit here would be on a day of non-admittance?

All these questions were flowing freely through my mind when suddenly a voice said, "Do you want to go into the cemetery?"

I looked up to see that a man of Latin-American appearance was addressing me.

"Oh yes please, can you help me get in there?"

"I am a mortician and I'm on my way to work there. Please follow me."

Never had I been so grateful to have such help when I needed it most. I followed the man to the unlocked side entrance. Positioning the yarmulke on my head I asked, "Can you please tell me where the Hebron section is? I am seeking row 7 space 28."

"It's over there behind that range of trees," he replied.

I thanked the man profusely and proceeded in the general direction of the trees, which were a considerable distance away. Behind them was a bewildering proliferation of headstones, all laid out horizontally. At intervals the various denominations of the Jewish religion were indicated.

Climbing a hill, I headed towards a gigantic building which must have been some kind of temple. against the background of the mountains and with the shimmering heat distorting the skyline, it almost looked like a mirage.

This was a distraction to the task in hand and it really was not the time or the place to engage in daydreams. Convinced that this was not where my father would be, I made an about turn and began to walk back down the tarmacked slope. Before me in the distant heat-haze lay the outline of Hollywood Hills and the suburbs of Los Angeles. To the left and to the right were more headstones, all laid horizontally but these were not of the right denomination.

I had been to a couple of Jewish cemeteries in the UK. Golders Green in North London in particular had fascinated me, not only for the various designs of the monuments but because of the famous names interred there. Here in Eden Memorial Park, every single gravestone was laid flat and had identical dimensions and features. It was in perfect order.

There was no one else in this cemetery. This was hardly a surprise bearing in mind the locked and chained gates, but this heightened the surreal atmosphere. My inner voice was saying to me: "Norm, you have come all this way, done all this research, made all this effort - you are not going to fail now".

Then at last I spotted a notice saying "Hebron section" (I learned later that Hebron meant Hebrew). Carefully locating row 7, I moved slowly along to number 28 and came face to face with my father's headstone for the very first time in my life.

Below a Hebrew inscription was the name

ISADORE JOSEPH SCHWARTZ
beloved husband, son and brother
1922 - 1966

Between the two dates was the star of David, and at the bottom was another Hebrew inscription. At long last the mystery of "Joseph Schwartz" had been unlocked and was there in front of me. Here was the evidence of who he really was and what had happened to him.

Significantly, the inscription read "beloved husband, son and brother". There was no mention of "father". It seemed that his secret had been taken to the grave.

A temporary paralysis come over me at this strange witnessing of my father's final resting place. Kneeling down, I began to talk to my father. First I forgave him for abandoning us and then asked, "Why are you here in your grave?" It did not seem fair that his life had been so short, and without the success that he had anticipated in the post-war years.

After a few moments I regained my composure. I took two items from my travel bag and placed them on his headstone. The first was the small bunch of artificial lilies Norma-Jean had suggested; the second was a framed photograph of my mother and me, taken in London circa 1970. I had inscribed a message alongside the photograph:

> ISADORE JOSEPH SCHWARTZ - FOR THE
> FREEDOM OF EUROPE, THANK YOU.
> YOUR LOVING SON, NORMAN.

Using my camera's automatic timer, I took a picture of myself kneeling by the grave. Then I took images of the two graves to the right, those of Philip and Charlotte Schwartz, Joe's parents and my paternal grandfather and grandmother.

I washed my hands in the fountain and left by the side entrance. It was time to head back to San Fernando. Once again the heat was blistering and I called in to a petrol station for a cold drink. My thoughts wandered back to the cemetery; "Beloved husband, son and brother". Even in death my father had kept the secret of my existence.

As a teenager I had imagined that my father's grave had been in a quiet corner of a foreign field in Europe. Instead I had found it in a Californian valley with palm trees and the outline of Beverley Hills and Hollywood shimmering in the far distance.

Back at San Fernando station, it would be some 45 minutes before the southbound train would arrive to take me back to Glendale. The heat was still rising when suddenly I heard the tinkling of a bell. Looking around, I observed a man standing alongside what could best be described as a three-wheeled hand trolley. On this trolley lay a vast array of confectionery items but, most importantly, there was ice cream!

Never have I enjoyed a coconut lolly on a stick so much. It was almost as though someone had brought me some kind of reward for my mini-ordeal in the sun.

On my return to Glendale it was time to shower, change clothes and seek out Niv Goren at the Americana. I needed to have a translation of the inscription on my father's headstone and assumed that Niv, being an Israeli, would be able to perform what to me seemed a straightforward task.

It turned out to be anything but straightforward. Niv visibly struggled with the image I had brought back on my camera and had to enlist the help of some other Jewish boys who were also working in the mall. None of them could provide a definitive translation. They recommended to me that I should consult a rabbi on my return home. I later did this and obtained the following translation:

Top Line: Yitzchak Yosef ben reb Yerucham Fischel
(Isaac Joseph son of Yerucham Fischel)
Bottom Line: Olav ha - shalom
(May he rest in peace).

Glendale is the adopted home of the highest percentage of Armenians in the United States (one in four of the population is of Armenian origin). It has a pleasant topography, with the San Gabriel mountains affording a Mediterranean-style backdrop to highlight the mixture of old and modern art deco buildings. Coupled with all this it has a well-known cemetery, Forest Lawn Memorial Park, where many famous residents and celebrities have their last resting places. However I had by now had quite enough of cemeteries, so a visit to Forest Lawn was definitely not on my itinerary.

Of far more interest were the comings and goings around Niv's stall in the Americana. There were many well-heeled tourists and, in addition, several people who could best be described as some of the more colourful local residents. As a form of bonus I got to know and exchange views on many topics with Niv. This provided some insight into the mind of a young Jewish person working in the United States. It all added up to quite a fun evening, and was just the type of light relief that was needed after such an arduous day.

All too soon it was over, and it was time to return to my hotel and prepare for the next day's early morning departure.

Glancing out of the aircraft window as the plane climbed high in the sky above Los Angeles, I wondered how long the picture and flowers would remain on my father's grave.

Would an attendant come along and remove them forthwith? (I was to learn later that what I had done was against

Jewish religious protocol). Would someone come along and read my message and wonder about the contradiction in fatherhood status?

I simply hoped that someone would come along and see that I cared. Most of all I hoped that they would see that my mother and father were together again in spirit.

It was as if bereavement, mourning, celebration of a person's life and the confirmation of my missing identity had all taken place in a brief few hours of events and meetings.

Back home in Wales, I had come home with several items and effects. A host of photographs of my father, a wartime 78 rpm recording of his voice, a lot more knowledge than when I had left and, the inevitable, obligatory, jet-lag!

I began to look through the cache of photographs I had returned with, and one in particular caught my eye. It showed my father and his brother Leonard posing carefully in the company of their father, Philip Schwartz. It reminded me of one of my earliest recollections of being in front of a camera. I was five years of age and it came after a journey along the Romney, Hythe and Dymchurch miniature railway in Kent. With the train having terminated at the Hythe depot, a man with a camera then appeared offering to sell copies of posed photographs. My mother readily agreed to this offer and I was placed in the cabin of the miniature steam train. I remember this event vividly and recall how the photographer's attention to my posing position was a rare occasion in my world when few adults would show interest in me.

The eventual picture turned out to be a very nice one, even though I seemed to bearing the expression of a "little boy lost". Looking now at the Schwartz family picture, the facial resemblance of my father's to mine at a similar age was absolutely unmistakable!

After a few days settling down I managed to locate a professional audio company in York who would be able to convert the 78 rpm recording to compact disc. To say that it would be interesting to hear my father's voice for the first and only time would be something of an understatement. It would not necessarily reveal any more information, but would give some impression of the voice my mother would have heard all those years ago.

I emailed to LeAnn in MI some of the pictures I had brought home and had the return observation "interesting to see some photos of Joe as a grown man". The vast majority of these pictures had been taken at a military base somewhere in England. The question now was - where was the base?

For many years I had mistakenly thought my father had been an airman in a bomber crew and would therefore have been based somewhere in East Anglia. Now I knew differently; Theron Johns had told me that he belonged to the 437th Troop Carrier Group. Visits to some of Cardiff's main bookshops failed to come up with anything other than publications about bomber crews and ground forces. This was disappointing, as almost all my newly-acquired photos had the names of the personnel written (in distinctive "Joseph Schwartz" style) on the back of each picture.

A few days later I casually typed "437th troop carrier group" into Google. As is normal in these quests, a host of web pages appeared on the screen and I went to the usually reliable Wikipedia to learn more. I received the usual bombardment of information, but it was only a matter of minutes before I located a pointer to direct me to the 437th's history. Apparently they (who were, even now, a total mystery to me) had been based at a place called Ramsbury in Wiltshire. The unit was part of the

United States 9th Air Force and had arrived there during February 1944. They had been based at Ramsbury for approximately one year, then departed on the 25th February 1945 to a French mainland airfield near the town of Coulomniers, 25 miles east of Paris. The primary aircraft assigned to the group was the C-47. Their main operation in the theatre of war was to transport paratroopers and tow gliders in airborne operations which included combat zones. Drops of vital supplies of food, fuel, medicine and ammunition were also part of their duties. When cessation of hostilities permitted they would evacuate the wounded, prisoners of war and displaced persons.

I could not place exactly where Ramsbury might be, but I consulted the atlas and soon located it. The nearest town was Hungerford, some three miles away, and the railway station was right on the main line to London which terminated at Paddington Station. During the war my mother lived and worked in the Notting Hill area of London, which is very close to Paddington.

Everything in the profile leading to my mother and father meeting was falling into place now, and not with too much effort other than typing at a keyboard.

I realised that in 1953 I had actually lived some 15 miles away from Ramsbury. Back then my mother had worked as a cook for a retired British Army Colonel who owned the Mill House in the tiny village of West Hendred. We had lived in the servants' quarters of Mill House for a year, and I had attended the village primary school.

This was around 1953, the coronation year of the new monarch, Queen Elizabeth II. To commemorate this event, all schoolchildren were given souvenir mugs. Excitedly running around the schoolroom with my new possession, I managed to stumble and break it. A shard from it pierced my palm, causing pain and not a few tears. A replacement mug and lots of fruit jelly eventually brought matters back to normality on an otherwise joyful occasion. Today I have a permanent scar on my left palm across one of my "lifelines". It does not actually say "1953", but I know what it means. How bizarre to think that back at that time I would be only some half an hour's bus ride from the scene of my father's wartime service with all its triumphs and traumas.

Having now identified Ramsbury geographically, it was logical to then Google that name again and see what might be uncovered. Sure enough another sub-heading came up which attracted me: "Ramsbury at War". Here was a welter of information compiled by a local author called Roger Day. It was almost too much to absorb at once. There was line after line of itemised detail about the various operations that had been carried out in the dark days of World War II. Alongside the text were various pictures of the wartime residents of this base. All were identified and acknowledged. I looked carefully for any image of my father, unlikely perhaps, but you never know.

Then a section about "The Invasion of Southern France" came up. A picture of aircrew who had been forced to "ditch" in the sea just off Land's End appeared on my computer screen. The plane bore the inscription "Terror of the Ozarks". This meant nothing to me, so I moved back to the crew photograph. I read the inscription underneath the image which listed the names involved: "S/Sgt Isadore Schwartz, T/Sgt Douglas Mitchell..." I stopped reading and did another take. The most prominent name now visible to me was "S/Sgt Isadore Schwartz".

I stared at the screen in disbelief. Looking back at me was my father lined up with the four other members of his crew, in a pose that reminded me of an opening act at the London Palladium Theatre.

This to me was simply incredible. Years and years of searching and hoping and now, with a few clicks of a computer mouse, here was the evidence of where my father had been in England, who he had worked with and the military operations undertaken.

My mind was made up. I would contact the author and source of all this information, Roger Day, to find out more and hopefully arrange a meeting and visit to Ramsbury.

However, as if to counteract all this new-found euphoria, I then received an email from Scott John's wife Paula in California. Aunt Ruth had been taken ill and admitted to hospital. Everyone over there, particularly Scott, was very concerned. Fortunately her condition was now stable.

I called Paula for an update and to say how sorry I was that this had happened. I did not want anything unforeseen to happen to my aunt, and wondered if I had been responsible in any way for her condition. Reassurance came back that this was not the case. Aunt Ruth had apparently been in hospital with this type of complaint on a couple of previous occasions.

Meantime LeAnn had been busy on my behalf and discovered some revealing data on the Ellis Island website. It showed details of the original entry into the United States of my paternal grandfather, Philip Schwartz.

Aged just 15, he was listed as Fischel Schwartz. In 1904 he had travelled overland from his home in the Galicia region of Poland to the port of Hamburg, Germany. From there he had sailed to America on board the SS *Patricia*. Travelling with him were two other members of the Schwartz family, his 11-year-old brother Leibisch and 17-year-old sister Pesche. She is registered in the "record of detained Alien Passengers" with the reason given as "brother and sister". This probably occurred when they had been separated during the inspection and registration process in the immigration hall.

Once reunited, their final destination was to be the home of a brother, Aaron Schwartz, who was living in the Borough of Brooklyn, New York City. Aaron was one of the first family members to enter America in 1902. This little trio had made the long sea voyage to a foreign land unaccompanied, quite a courageous achievement back then, as they would not have been fluent in English. This did not in itself carry the tag of a revelation, but nevertheless gave me a path to an even deeper analysis of my newly-found ancestors.

Now the immediate priority was to find out more about my father's military life, which was something that unlocked a feeling of admiration in me. Compared to previous searches, locating Roger Day's telephone number was a walk in the park. It was not long before I came to be explaining to Roger about my newly-found interest in Ramsbury and the personal link associated with it.

I emailed some of the pictures I had brought back from California to him, and they brought an immediate response. Roger sent back information as to their military location and crew assignment. Then he afforded me an unexpected bonus by giving me the address of the man who had been the captain of my father's plane, William M. Thompson Lt. Col USAF (Ret). Apparently William "Tommie" Thompson was alive and well and residing in the Texan city of San Antonio.

Now San Antonio is the location of the famous battle of the Alamo in 1836 and something I was familiar with both on the "silver screen" and from a visit there way back in 1980. Using the details of Tommie's address I quickly located his telephone number.

It was with particular pleasure and anticipation that I made the call to him on May 30th 2010. This date is significant, as it is US Memorial Day, when the country pays homage to all deceased military service personnel.

I dialled the number, the ringing tone began and someone in San Antonio answered. "Hello, I am calling from the United Kingdom" I said. "Is it possible please to speak to William Thompson?"

In an instant I was talking to him. "Excuse me sir" I said, "but did you fly a plane called the Terror of the Ozarks in the Second World War?" He said he had, and I began to enquire about the radio operator of the plane.

"Isadore? Oh yes he was my overweight radio operator," he said. "A jolly fine fellow".

This was enthralling. I was actually conversing with the captain of my father's plane, who clearly remembered him. Now I had to identify the reason for my interest.

At first Tommie seemed a little nonplussed at what I was telling him. Receiving an unexpected long-distance telephone call from someone claiming to be a relative of your former WWII aircrew would be confusing for anyone!

I asked him to confirm his address and promised to write giving more specific details as to how I came to be contacting him from "out of the blue".

This call was yet another landmark in my search, though in effect the search had reached a conclusion, if in some respects a disappointing one.

The next few days were spent analysing my recent discoveries, and this regenerated my enthusiasm for discovering more about my father's background, both militarily and genealogically. It was going to be a busy summer, one full of discoveries, diversions, introductions and reminiscences.

CHAPTER FIFTEEN

A VOICE FROM THE PAST

I didn't have long to wait for my reply from Tommie Thompson. First came an email which described my father as a "personable and jolly fellow who was dedicated to his responsibilities". Coming from the captain of his plane this was some accolade, even if it did nothing to explain his peacetime lack of responsibility. A letter, said Tommie, would follow.

It was not long before it arrived and the tone was very friendly. Enclosed was an original copy of a edition of the news sheet "Flaps Up". This USAAF mini-journal dedicated half of its space to serious articles relating to the progress of the war. The remainder contained details of amusing incidents and anecdotes about everyday airbase activities and incidents. Published around Christmas 1944, this particular edition featured a list of fictitious "awards". Tommie had underlined the details of an award to "Izzy Schwartz" for "services to chow".

Back in California Theron had mentioned to me that "all the Schwartzes were good eaters". The various pictures of my father had left me with no doubt about that either.

When I had talked on the telephone to Tommie I had asked him whether he could tell me any details about my father from his personal experience. Tommie had explained that after combat missions and debriefing, the crews would go their respective ways. Being an officer meant that he had not had the opportunity to form any kind of friendship through mutual social activities, so I had to be content with what he had sent me.

The letter finished with the words: "Norman, your father was to be admired for his dedication and service to our country and his participation in World War II".

My father was emerging as a larger-than-life character in every sense of the word. I felt a slight mellowing of my anger towards him as these details of military life began to unfold. It was as if I had been retold the many WWII things I had read or seen on television, in the cinema or on the radio. John Wayne, Audie Murphy, Robert Mitchum et al had portrayed vivid images of patriotism, bravery, inventiveness and self-sacrifice the likes of which I had never tired of hearing about. Now a personal connection with all that had been established. Quite simply I was spellbound.

Now I needed to visit the airbase in Ramsbury from which my father had flown on operations. I contacted Roger Day and arranged to meet up with him in a few weeks' time. He promised to arrange a walking tour on which we could inspect what remained of the base.

In the meantime the CD conversion of the wartime recording of my father's voice arrived back from the studios of David Grant in York. I felt a heightened sense of anticipation as I loaded the disc onto my stereo system for the first time. The original recording had been made in Sioux Falls, South Dakota, at a training camp in 1943. At that time Isadore Schwartz was 21 years old. Servicemen were each allotted a recording time of 90 seconds per side, which left precious little time for an audio masterpiece.

I pushed the "play" button and waited to hear my father's voice for the first time. The slightly frenetic pitch of his voice reminded me of James Cagney as he went on to describe his impressions of life in and around Sioux Falls. Time constraints and censorship had kept it short, so it was over almost before it had begun, and it told me very little. Nevertheless it was both momentous and surreal to listen to my father for the first and only time. The realisation that my mother had heard this voice heightened the pathos.

Welcome news now came through from California. Aunt Ruth had returned home from hospital and was making a good recovery. During the summer of 2010 we would have many lengthy telephone conversations. She was a night owl, while I was an early riser. This combination worked well in tandem with the eight-hour time difference between Wales and California.

On June 22nd 2010 I set out for Ramsbury to meet Roger Day. Reading from his website, I had learned that my father had been an enlisted aircrew member of the 437th's 85th Squadron, which had arrived in Ramsbury during February 1944. Roger had now very kindly offered to give up part of his afternoon to show me around the site of the former airbase and surrounding buildings.

Roger's expert eye could, in an instant, transform an abandoned building foundation, a break in the trees or disturbed earthworks into a WWII operational military site. We must have covered a couple of miles during the walk and it enabled me to appreciate the vast distance between these buildings and the actual airfield. It was little wonder that a fleet of bicycles used to be employed to get the servicemen to the runway in double-quick time!

For the final part of this fascinating tour we drove to the scene of a nearby airfield at Membury. In the present day some of the original hangar buildings are in commercial use, but the runway itself is intersected by the M4 motorway and services facilities.

Today most people calling in at the M4 Membury services are unaware of the historical significance of the location. Outside the westbound complex, on a grass verge, an aircraft propeller stands mounted vertically on a concrete plinth inscribed with a dedication to all the aircrew who operated from there during WWII. It was from here, on June 5th 1944 at 2300 hours, the C-47 transporter plane named "Terror of the Ozarks" took off en route for the Cherbourg peninsula in Northern Brittany. The plane and its crew had been transferred from Ramsbury to Membury on the 29th May. On board with the aircrew that evening were the paratroopers of the 377th Parachute Field Artillery 101st Airborne. They were equipped for combat and standing by to parachute out of the plane into the darkness and drop down to the designated zone on the French mainland.

The radio operator for this flight was Isadore Joseph Schwartz. He was about to have a busy night on this historic mission. Everyone on board now faced a journey by air which was full of apprehension and real danger. This was it – this was the "big one". The long-awaited invasion of Europe had begun.

Once in the air they would become part of two serials (formations) comprising 90 aircraft. Upon reaching the French mainland, they would encounter blinding searchlights beamed at them from the ground, accompanied by tracer bullet fire. Following successful discharge of the paratroopers, the "Terror of the Ozarks" then returned safely back to a base in England.

The experience of "walking in the footsteps of the 437th" remained a lasting memory of an interesting and even surreal afternoon. The knowledge that I had been to the scene of my father's wartime experience of the UK was enthralling.

Not long after this event, Roger put me in touch with a surviving member of the 437th who lived in Sacramento, California. Donald P Bolce had been in the same squadron (85th) as my father and performed the same tasks as a radio operator. After receiving my initial response he quickly wrote back giving me some details of my father's military duties, military serial number and even his last home address in Los Angeles.

After receiving this I decided to speak to him by telephone. The conversation was a little convoluted due to my fast speech and Don's hearing problems. With a little assistance from his wife Bonnie, we did however, manage to make ourselves understood. Don told me that his wartime career paralleled that of my father's. It read like a resume of the war in Europe: the invasion of Italy, the invasion of Southern France, D-Day, Normandy, Operation Market Garden, the invasion of Germany across the Rhine. All this involvement concerned the airborne activities of the 437th.

Don told me that my father had been a "clever, warm, friendly guy" who could mimic British accents. One speciality was Winston Churchill. Don told me that during operations my father never showed any fear - nor did Winston Churchill.

Don and Bonnie promised to send further information which they felt would help me get to know my father better. They then put me in touch with another person who had a great interest in the history of the group. This was Nottinghamshire-based Neil Stevens.

Neil's connection with the 437th's operations at Ramsbury had begun at a very early age. He had grown up in nearby Marlborough and his father had always related his own keen interest in WWII to him. This had inspired Neil to become a reservist in the British army. When he was 18 years old he and his unit had camped out for the night on the remains of RAF Ramsbury.

The date of this event was significant. It was June 6th, 1986. The realisation that he was there on the 42nd anniversary of D-Day inspired further interest. From that time onwards Neil took an active part in preserving the memory of the 437th's activities and became their official group historian. Neil now provided me with a link to two other former members of the 437th, Lewis "Lew" Shank and James "Jim" Lyons. He also afforded me some interesting insights into the wartime routines at Ramsbury. When I sent him some pictures of me and my father taken at similar ages in our youth his comment was: "Good God. It's like two twins who have been separated at birth!"

I then followed up on Neil's information. Lew Shank was pleased to hear from me. Like most people, he had no idea that former colleague "Izzy " Schwartz had had a son.

Jim Lyons had a few problems talking by phone, as he was just recovering from the debilitating effects of a stroke, but nevertheless it was good to speak to him.

"I often used to see Schwartz on Saturday nights in Swindon" he told me (Swindon is 12 miles from Ramsbury). Jim did not enlarge on that statement. Suffice to say that, like most young servicemen he was not in town looking to join the local chess club!

Jim went on to describe Neil Stevens as the "Godfather of the 437th". Neil had, he told me, been instrumental in getting a memorial placed in the Kennet valley near to the spot where members of the group had perished in a training accident. He had also been active with fundraising and assisting in reunion events.

These new contacts had all cascaded in within a matter of days - something which even a few years ago would not have been possible. The digital age is good at giving up secrets.

The next piece of information came through by mail from Don. He sent me a copy of an article taken from an August 18th 1962 edition of the *Stars and Stripes* journal. It was a full-page spread on the annual reunion of the 437th Troop Carrier Group which had taken place that year in Washington DC. There was a group photo of eighteen smartly-attired members of the group, with individual identification in an adjacent column. There, on the extreme left of the centre row, wearing a light summer suit, a bow-tie and a smile, stood a certain I. J. Schwartz. His features were unmistakable, and he looked a picture of good health.

Whereas all the others were dressed more formally, my father stood out as the confident showman, at ease with himself and the rest of the world. It was difficult to imagine that within four years he would be gone from the world.

Seeing this picture, I was torn between fascination and resentment, for I recalled that at this time in 1962, life had been difficult for my mother and me.

Towards the end of August 2010, a small but symbolic event occurred that served to underline my new family identity. Adam Johns, the son of cousin Scott, had mentioned to me in California that he might do a vacational course at Cambridge University the following summer. Adam said that if he did get to Cambridge he would try to take time to make a visit to South Wales and meet up with me for weekend.

Sure enough he managed to keep his promise, and we arranged to rendezvous at Cardiff Central railway station, from where I would take him to his pre-booked student accommodation. I managed to show him the sights and attractions of the area. This included a whistle-stop tour of the capital city, the South Wales valleys and the beautiful Gower coast.

When I showed him where I lived in Caerphilly and Adam first stepped over the threshold of my house, it was to me a highly significant and symbolic act. For the first time ever, a member of the Schwartz lineage had taken the time and trouble to come to my home, and in so doing underline acceptance of me as a genuine member of their family.

Indeed Adam's visit had further significance in underlining my identity. He was the first blood relative ever to set foot in my home. The nomadic trails my mother and I had followed, combined with the illegitimacy of my birth, had always presented formidable obstacles to such a meeting. I can only speculate that my mother would have been delighted at such a demonstration of loyalty from Adam.

In July 2014 I was able to repay this in some way by attending Adam's wedding to his long-time girlfriend Ariana Curtiss on the beach at Coronado, San Diego, California.

Some time after his return to California, Adam sent me an email saying that of all the places he had visited during his time in the United Kingdom, South Wales had been the best. He concluded by thanking me for being such an "awesome cousin". Praise indeed. I was delighted by his generous response.

Shortly before Christmas 2010 Neil Stevens got in touch, telling me that he was due to attend a conference in Cardiff. He suggested a meeting, which I was very pleased to arrange. The temperature was sub-zero as I made the short walk to Caerphilly town centre to seek out Neil in his car. Sure enough he was there waiting, and lowering his window, he handed me a photograph. It was the same picture of the "Terror of the

Ozarks" aircrew I had brought back from California. This copy however was of superior quality. I thought how bizarre it was that after travelling on a 10,000 mile round trip to get such an image I was now being handed the same picture just one mile from my house! Needless to say I was very grateful that Neil was able to present me with such a precious gift.

We went for an evening meal at a local pub, where our discussion centred upon the 437th and the complexities of the wartime operations at Ramsbury. Neil, who was originally from that area, had always had a great interest in the group's history and had been proactive in communicating with the veterans and their families. This interesting evening produced more knowledge of my father's wartime past.

I reflected on this and realised that there were still some more important milestones left to achieve. I had to meet Aunt Marian in Philadelphia; I had to see for myself what Altoona PA was like; and I had to find out more about my father's wife Shirley and her daughter Beth, including their possible whereabouts.

But before I could fulfil these ambitions, a door closed in my face. On Monday, December 13th 2010, an email came through from Scott Johns. His mother Ruth had passed away at sundown the previous evening after a brief illness. This news greatly saddened me. A firm relationship had been forming between my aunt and me. I knew my grief would be nothing compared to that felt by her immediate family. All I could do was send my condolences to them. A family link had been broken too soon after it had been forged.

Neither of my two aunts had been able to tell me what had happened to Shirley Schwartz and her daughter Beth after my father's death. I needed to solve this puzzle in order to extract further information about my father's life. I had discussed this conundrum with LeAnn, who suggested that these people might have some of my father's personal possessions. Naturally I wanted to obtain some physical token of his life - perhaps a ring, a medal or a personal diary. The value was immaterial; it was the connection that was important.

In January 2011 LeAnn emailed to say that she would be visiting Los Angeles as part of her work. She hoped to be able to find time to visit Los Angeles Public Library and inspect the city directories for the years 1960-1965 (the time when my father had lived there). If she could find him listed there, there was a chance that spouse Shirley would also be registered. There would then be a chance of finding a post-February 1966 forwarding address.

After her LA visit, LeAnn informed me that her resulting research had yielded three mentions of men called Isadore Joseph Schwartz, one of whom had lived in Tarzana, LA. The Tarzana address matched the one that Don Bolce had previously sent me. Alas, there was no mention of Shirley or Beth. This, for all intents and purposes, seemed like a dead end.

Now it was my turn to take a little initiative. On the internet I caught site of an advertisement for a website called archives. com. It advertised access to past editions of US newspapers that had digitised their records. I decided that although it might lead nowhere, the $30 three-month trial period afforded me plenty of time to exploit and interpret any information gained. I might, after all, gain some clues relevant to the search for Shirley Schwartz.

I paid the fee and started to surf. First I typed in search for "Shirley Schwartz Los Angeles". I was swamped with results. I then narrowed down the criteria by adding the timeline "1960-

65" and the word "Tarzana". That too failed to produce anything conclusive. I logged off, thinking I had wasted $30, and retired for the evening.

Sometimes when you sleep on things, you find a new source of inspiration the following day. The next morning I thought it might be worth temporarily forgetting about Shirley and instead look for "Isadore Joseph Schwartz". I typed in "newspapers in Altoona PA" and added his name. An article in the *Altoona Mirror* from 1932 appeared, listing my father's poetry recital in the local synagogue. I thought maybe Archives. com was not such a bad buy after all!

Then something came up to prove that it was an excellent buy. Staying with the *Altoona Mirror*, a page from Friday, February 11th 1966 appeared. I began looking for mentions of Isadore Joseph Schwartz. Under a column headed, "CITY NATIVE EXPIRES IN LOS ANGELES" I read:

Isadore Joseph Schwartz, a former Altoona resident, died Feb 3rd in the West Los Angeles VA Hospital after an extended illness. His death was attributed to kidney failure.

He was born in Altoona Sept 22 1922, a son of Philip and Charlotte (Fassler) Schwartz, attended Miller Grade School, DS Keith Junior High and Altoona High School, from where he graduated in 1940.

Following graduation he attended the Clearfield Aviation Institute, then went to Olmstead Airbase at Middleton to work.

He enlisted in the Army Air Corps on Nov 3rd 1942 and received training in Fresno, California, Scott Field, ILL and Sioux Falls SD as a radio operator and mechanic on a twin-engined C-47 transport plane.

His crew was active in transporting men and supplies during the Italian campaign in 1943 and the Normandy invasion in 1944.

Following the siege at Bastogne his plane was in the first group to carry supplies to Americans trapped during the Battle of the Bulge. Many wounded GIs were removed by his unit, the 437th Troop Carrier Command. The unit took paratroopers and loaded gliders into France during the Normandy invasion and North Africa previously.

Once his airplane developed trouble and had to be ditched in the English Channel. He sent out the SOS and a British freighter picked up the entire crew.

While his outfit was based near Rome following Italy's defeat in 1943, he attended an audience with Pope Pius XII. He always recalled how impressive that was to him and the other GIs with him.

He was a Staff Sergeant and was discharged from the Air Corps after three years of service. He took up study at the Philadelphia Wireless School to get his civilian license as a radio engineer. He also attended the University of Michigan for two years of aeronautical engineering at Ann Arbor, Mich.

Mr Schwartz was a radio engineer and announcer for WVAM radio station and was employed there for nine and a half years.

In October 1959 he went to live in Los Angeles, working for RCA, and later entered his own business of sound recordings.

On August 18th 1960, Mr Schwartz was united in marriage with Shirley Kaya of Kalamazoo, Mich, by Rabbi Joseph Schwartz of Benton Harbour, Mich.

They resided at 5332, Veloz Ave, Tarzana, Calif.

He is survived by his wife, a step-daughter Beth at the home, his parents Mr and Mrs Philip Schwartz of Los Angeles, also two former Altoonians: two sisters, Mrs Ruth Johns of Orange, Calif, and Mrs Marian Garfinkel of Philadelphia, and a brother, Leonard H of Altoona.

He was a member of the Ohavel Yosher Synagogue while in Altoona and of many veterans' organisations.

Funeral services and interment were held in Los Angeles.

I read the newspaper article several times. It had a strange aura of unreality about it. Was this really my father? All the information I could wish for was there, bar one item. When it came to "He is survived by", a name was missing - mine!

Now, all of a sudden, I knew the apparent home town and state of the elusive Shirley. Although I hoped that I would find her alive and well, the obvious passage of time meant I had to adopt the worst-case scenario.

I began to search for her in the United States Death Index for Michigan State, and found her. She had passed away in 1994. She did not appear to have remarried after my father's death. Wanting to be absolutely sure, I made efforts to obtain a copy of the death certificate. The few photos I had seen of her gave me a good chance of estimating her year of birth with reasonable accuracy.

After telephoning several local governmental departments, I finally found the right one. It was the County Register of Deeds in Kalamazoo. I began: "Good morning, I am trying to obtain a copy of the death certificate of a Mrs Schwartz, social security no. ********, formerly of Kalamazoo, born circa early to mid-1920s". The official on the end of the line quickly brought up a microfilm record which matched the details given.

"Yes, I appear to have it here, Shirley Schwartz". He read out the home address and added: "Would you like to know the name of the informant?"

"Yes please. "

"It's a Mrs Beth Copp. "The home address was read out and I hastily noted it down.

"Would you like to order a certificate, or is that sufficient information?"

Sufficient information? It was a veritable gold mine. The names given to me matched exactly those given to me by my aunts, ie Shirley and Beth.

I thanked the helpful official in the register office and told him that I had enough detail. Provided Beth's address was unchanged from 1994, there was now every chance of contacting her. The mystery of what had happened to the missing duo had now been unravelled. They had left California and returned to their home state of Michigan.

I still had to meet Aunt Marian in person and needed to firm up arrangements to do this. I remembered my friends in Lancaster Pennsylvania, Bruce and Charol Thompson.
I had stayed with them back in 1982 under the Friendship Force exchange scheme. We had remained in touch ever since then and maybe they would be willing to assist once more.

I contacted them and their reaction was both typically generous and immediate.. They would be only too happy to help. We arranged dates for spring 2011 which would allow sufficient time for me both to see Aunt Marian in Philadelphia and visit my father's hometown, Altoona.

CHAPTER SIXTEEN

IN MY FATHER'S
FOOTSTEPS

The discovery of my father's obituary in the 1965 *Altoona Mirror* archive seemed to finally lay to rest the letter allegedly written from St Louis in which my father had told of his forthcoming marriage to a heavily pregnant Mary. So it was with some anticipation that I prepared a letter to Beth Copp in Portage, Kalamazoo, giving brief details about myself and my father's wartime romance with my mother. I enclosed several photographs illustrating my likeness to her late stepfather.

Now I could only hope for a response. I had been in this situation before! I was hoping that the anticipated reply would be sympathetic. Perhaps Beth would still have some item of my father's personal possessions and would be willing to pass one or two of them on to me. It would not have to be an expensive item – a driving licence, a diary or a pair of cufflinks would do.

While waiting, I firmed up my plans to visit the Thompsons in Pennsylvania and sent Aunt Marian details of my arrival and departure dates. Her response didn't come across as exactly enthusiastic, but I remained hopeful that when my time of departure came nearer, a more positive reaction would ensue. In any event, one way or another I was determined to see what she looked like in real life, even if it meant gatecrashing one of the Ijengar Yoga classes she frequently conducted in Philadelphia.

By a strange quirk of fate I had been in Philadelphia some 29 years previously with Charol Thompson when we had been to sightsee the "City of Brotherly Love". Marian and I might even have passed each other on the street without so much as a second look. Such is the hand of fate, a phenomenon which my father had referred to in his "St Louis letter".

Besides simply wanting to trace my father, I had always nurtured the ambition to attain American citizenship. Although many members of the Transatlantic Children's Enterprise have achieved this, the application procedure is both long and complex. You have to prove conclusively that you are the child of the GI concerned. Evidence in the form of official documentation is mandatory. Among the requirements are the serviceman's birth certificate and, should he have died in the interim, the death certificate.

I needed to have these certificates, so first I requested the assistance of LeAnn. She would be instrumental in obtaining the death certificate in the form of an informational copy. Next I contacted Aunt Marian for her assistance in providing the birth certificate. Regulations stipulate that only a blood relative can apply for a birth certificate, and up to now I was an unproven relative. I would be unable to make a direct application myself.

My father's death certificate was more than just a form to me. It would reveal the actual medical cause of death. This could give me an indication of any conditions that I myself might have inherited.

Another stipulation of the US Department of State is the provision of the soldier's honourable discharge papers. These documents would serve to confirm my father's identity and the fact that he had served in World War II.

Once again I wrote off to the National Personnel Records Center in St Louis (how strange it was that St Louis continued to be part of a link in all this). My letter was addressed to Management Analyst Niels J. Zussblatt PhD. Niels was the official in the NPRC who over the years had dealt directly with the many applications from GI children seeking information on their father's service records. Over a period of many years this man has become the equivalent of an additional tier of support for members of the Transatlantic Children's Enterprise. His outstanding dedication to duty and attention to detail have resulted in countless people being able to find and establish contact with their biological GI fathers. He has received many written requests from myself, over the years and always they were of the same format, eg: "Please send a copy of the final pay check and any other relevant details and information for SCHWARTZ, Joseph". So it was with great pleasure and no little confidence that this time, my request to Dr. Zussblatt was in relation to:

Veteran's Name: SCHWARTZ, Isadore

SSN/SN 13145625

My letter concluded with a brief note of thanks to Niels for all his past assistance and his humanity, which were, as always, deeply appreciated. A certified copy of the replacement certificate came back almost by return of post (the originals had perished in the great fire of 1973). Another chapter had finally been closed.

Now winter was finally releasing its icy grip and the time came to once again "go west" across the Atlantic. I would visit the Thompson family, meet Aunt Marian and go and see for myself that mysterious town called Altoona.

Shortly before my planned departure for Pennsylvania on

March 11th, a hand-written letter arrived from Michigan. It was from Beth Copp, and was written in a pleasant, informative style. Both my aunts and my father's military colleagues had no previous knowledge of my existence. In her letter Beth confirmed that she too had not known about me, and was enthusiastic to know more. I felt the same way, and before long we were exchanging emails and telephone calls.

In my first telephone call to Beth I told her about my father's letters to my mother and what the St Louis letter had contained. Her reaction to this was instant. "Mr Spencer, it seems to me that you've been brushed under the carpet," she said. When it came to the result of my father's post-war actions, this was indeed the unpalatable truth.

Beth had been in her early teenage years when her mother married my father and did not have many memories of that time to recall. She did remember my father's insistence that his new wife and stepdaughter must attend the synagogue on a weekly basis. He had been very strict with her, and any out-of-school activities had a curfew rigorously imposed.

Shortly before my departure for Pennsylvania I received a call from Aunt Marian. She was looking forward to meeting me and suggested that on my arrival at Philadelphia airport, where I was to be met by Bruce and Charol Thompson, we should all go to her apartment for "high tea". This was too good an offer to refuse, although exactly what Aunt Marian's "high tea " would be was anyone's guess. To make things more authentic, I pledged to bring a suitable brand of tea of my own with me.

Since the devastating events of 9/11, US airports had been understandably slow in dealing with immigration queues, and my arrival in Philadelphia was no different. After some time I was reunited with Bruce and Charol, who proceeded to drive me into the centre of Philadelphia. For traffic signs and lane identification, this place is a motorist's nightmare, unless of course, you are a resident. Eventually we found our way to the street where my aunt's private apartment block was. At the reception desk we were asked to wait for a few minutes and then directed to the relevant floor.

As we rose in the elevator, I speculated about what the next few minutes would bring. Once again I would be coming face to face with one of my father's sisters – with someone who, until some fourteen months before, had had no idea that she had a nephew living in the United Kingdom.

In the gloomy corridor I could see the petite figure of Marian Garfinkel approaching. Her step was a slow, careful one but as soon as the light became more favourable, I was greeted by the words, "Hi, welcome. I can see that you are a Schwartz".

This eased the tension I had been feeling, though not the tiredness. I had been travelling for some 17 hours and only the adrenalin was keeping me awake.

"High Tea" really was that – a magnificent array of sandwiches, cakes and, of course tea. Charol was active with her camera and I remembered Norma-Jean's prompting – "Be sure you have a photograph taken with your aunt". This would be a vital piece of evidence when applying for US citizenship.

What was equally important was that there seemed a genuine family resemblance –something the authorities could not deny.

We spent a pleasant couple of hours together before it was time to head out to the Thompson abode in Millersville PA and a good night's sleep. What then followed was a week and a half of discovery, not just of the background of Isadore Joseph Schwartz but of the Thompson family and the history of

Pennsylvania State. It began with a tour of their residence, which was a converted farmhouse dating back to the seventeenth century.

There was the pleasure of seeing again their now grown-up son Chad (of 1982 tennis playing fame) and his sisters Melissa and Stephanie. Stephanie had not yet been born the last time I had set foot in Pennsylvania.

Now there was time to tour the surrounding countryside, observing the local Amish community going about their daily business and visiting the famous Pennsylvania Railroad Museum. Towards the end of the second week Bruce, Charol and I firmed up plans for a very important two-day trip to a town some three hours' drive from Millersville - Altoona. Now at last I would be able to see for myself what kind of town my father had grown up in, visit his former high school and locate the grave of my uncle, Leonard H Schwartz.

The drive to Altoona was entirely by freeway through tolls and tunnels. All the time one is aware of the steady climb up into a wide valley surrounded by wooded hills and interspersed with mountain streams. For two hours, with a brief stop, nothing of note could be seen until "ALTOONA" began to appear on the direction signs. I have to confess to feeling a tinge of excitement when first seeing this. Never in my wildest imagination had I anticipated going to the home town of the mysterious "Joseph Schwartz, 703 Church Street, Ann Arbor, Michigan, USA".

After what seemed an eternity, we entered the outskirts of Altoona. Charol commented that she could hear the excitement in my voice as we drew ever closer. I began to take a series of photographs, most of which captured the name "Altoona".

We exited the freeway and made our way into the

downtown area, parking on one of the main streets opposite the US Post Office on 11th Avenue. I got out of the vehicle, knelt down and touched the ground. The eagle has landed, I thought. Here I was standing on the same street where my father had once stood, breathing the same air and looking at the same buildings (excluding the obviously modern ones).

The plan for the two-day stay included going to see a former schoolmate of my father, Lou Bavarsky, in the hope that he might be able to recall some past times and events. Another plan was to locate the site of the family butcher's shop. According to the results of the 1930 census it had been located on 18th Street. All the original buildings on that street had long since been swept away and replaced by new ones, but it was still an ambition of mine to stand on approximately the same spot, pause, meditate and imagine what life must have been like there all those years ago.

We decided to separate for a while. Bruce, who had been doing the driving, drove away to find an outlet for a well-earned cup of coffee. Charol and I then began to walk along 11th Avenue towards the intersection with 18th Street.

The exact address of my grandfather's butcher's shop had been given as 1111 18th, which was also the home address the University of Michigan had for my father. Thanks to Google Earth I knew exactly where to go and stand – or so I thought. After about ten minutes we found the spot. It was now a customers' car park for an adjacent business complex. We took some photographs which would be useful in recalling that I had indeed visited the scene of many Schwartz family dramas and achievements.

Exploring the downtown area of Altoona, it soon became obvious that the mountain city had long since passed the high-water mark of success and prosperity and was in the throes of re-inventing itself. Its development had been based around railroad travel, communications and engineering, exploitation of mineral wealth and no little individual drive and enterprise. In the inter-war years it would have been exciting to behold, a bustling community with streetcars clanking along the streets and the ringing tills of the shops and department stores. The noise and pollution of the largest railroad workshop in the world would have provided a background to all this activity. Together they would have spelt employment and relative prosperity.

Now all around us lay deserted shops and vacant plots, interspersed with magnificent churches and temples and a truly magnificent cathedral. The decline of heavy industry coupled, with the advent of the out-of-town shopping mall, had brought the era of mass downtown shopping to an end. Now all around there was faded glory. Some noble efforts at restoration were being made to stem back the tide of decay. The similarity with certain parts of South Wales was uncanny, with the landscape, topography and back roads forming a mirror image.

It was time for some further sightseeing, and we left Altoona to view the famous railroad Horseshoe Curve, which lay a few miles beyond the city centre. Famous not only in Pennsylvania but all over the US, the curve had, during the Second World War, been on the list of targets designated for destruction by Hitler's Third Reich. From a personal point of view, there was no denying the fact that this landmark would have featured in my father's young life. The mountain-top communities of Cresson and Gallitzin had been mentioned by him during his brief Sioux Falls wartime recording session.

Our arrival at the curve proved to be a minor letdown. A notice proclaimed that the observation platform was closed until the Easter period. Was this going to stop me going to see what my father must have seen many times? Of course not! I soon discovered a gap in the security fencing and managed to squeeze through it. Scrambling up the steep embankment, I found myself level with the trackbed.

I made a quick photocall before descending safely. Then it was time to make the drive up the narrow winding mountain road to Cresson and Gallitzin. Endlessly the road ascended, twisting and turning through the mist.

Two thoughts kept going through my mind. First, that my father must have known this route very well and second, how very similar it was to the many mountain-top roads back home in South Wales.

Eventually we came to a plateau. Passing through Cresson and Gallitzin, it was obvious that this former coal mining area had fallen into bad times. We managed to find an "Irish Pub" for some sustenance. Inside, hanging on the walls, were many historical pictures of the area. This gave a good illustration of the sense of isolation about this community.

Night was falling as we ascended from our little tour, and we made plans for our second day in Altoona.

The next morning these were put into action. First came the visit to a local nursing home where Lou Bavarsky, one of my father's school pals, was now residing. Aunt Marian had revealed his name and said that he might be able to give me some information about my father's life. She warned, however, that it might prove problematic, as Mr Bavarsky was suffering from Alzheimer's disease.

It had taken a few phone calls to locate this gentleman, as he had moved from another institution. He was now at the Valley View nursing home on the outskirts of Altoona. A pleasant reception staff directed us to his room on the second floor. When we got there the room was empty, and we were quickly directed to the day room. There was Mr Bavarsky, in a wheelchair, watching television.

Charol introduced us and we shook his hand. I held up the document file I had brought. There were several pictures of my father for him to see but alas, they brought no response from Lou. I thought I caught a brief flicker of recognition when I showed him my father's graduation photograph, but alas another brief flicker was the only acknowledgement.

My knowledge of Alzheimer's disease is superficial to say the least, but the next forty-five minutes confirmed to me what a horrible affliction it is. Despite repeated attempts to gain a response from Mr Bavarsky, during this time nothing transpired and we left the home unrewarded.

I thought how difficult it must be for his family to have to endure this situation with their every visit. It was obvious from all the various greetings from family members that were posted around his room that they loved him very much.

Next on the agenda was a visit to the Agudath Achim Jewish Cemetery, which was on the outskirts of town. The mission was to locate the grave of my father's elder brother, Leonard, my uncle. During several of the telephone conversations with Aunt Marian the subject of Leonard had been touched upon several times. Of all the four Schwartz siblings he had been the only one to stay in his birthplace, Altoona, for his entire lifetime. He passed away there in 1986, aged 65.

During World War II Leonard had enlisted in the United States Army Infantry and risen to the rank of 2nd Lieutenant. On returning home he had established a pre-owned automobile business operated from premises on 18th Street adjacent to his parents' kosher butcher's shop. It seemed he had been a larger-than-life character. Indeed, from what Aunt Marian told me he had developed a rather domineering personality within the family home. This had led to friction between him and my father.

Due to the very demanding nature of operating a kosher meat service to the local Jewish community the Schwartz household had been a somewhat frenetic one. Indeed my Aunt had related to me that the only times my grandfather had found time to relax would have been on a Saturday, the Jewish Sabbath.

Having failed the previous day to find anyone at the synagogue to give any information about the opening times for the cemetery, there was a nagging doubt in my mind. I was afraid that I would once again be confronted by locked cemetery gates. I need not have worried. Our journey out of town took us on an upward route to a beautiful wooded valley and the cemetery itself, which was open for public access.

Unlike my visit to the cemetery in the San Fernando Valley, where the location of my father's grave had been pre-listed, this time I had no designated row or plot number to assist in finding my uncle's grave. What I did have was a feeling of a sixth sense, and an inner confidence that despite the many rows of monuments, I would find the location very quickly. With Charol assisting I soon found the grave, which lay in an elevated position underneath some pine trees.

"Rest in peace, Uncle Leonard, rest in peace," I whispered before placing a stone I had brought from Wales on the base of his monument. Lying there were four stones brought by previous visitors as evidence that he had not been entirely forgotten.

It was time to visit my father's former High School and

enquire about the availability of any archive material. I wanted to personally thank Diane, the secretary who had kindly sent me the graduation photosheet the previous year. The officials at the High School were more than accommodating, though unfortunately Diane was not present, having retired the previous year. To my surprise they produced a copy of my father's school report, while at the same time presenting me with a copy of the yearbook for 1940, his graduation year.

The yearbook was a very impressive item of memorabilia. It was in hardbound format with an abundance of visual material covering all aspects of the school's curriculum from academic to sports and from musical to scientific.

Isadore Schwartz was featured on one page as an active member of the school Physics Club, complete with group photo call. Standing poignantly at the front of the group was the unmistakable profile of Lou Bavarsky, who was clearly the "leader of the pack" when it came to wearing the very latest stylish clothes of that era.

I thanked the people at the High School for their kind assistance and we moved on to visit the nearby Baker Mansion. Originally the home of Ironmaster Elias Baker, this three-storey historical building was an impressive sight. Much to our disappointment it was not possible to tour the premises, but to counterbalance this, a useful contact was made. The official at the mansion put me in touch with the Blair County Genealogical Society, who were holding a meeting later that day at their headquarters in nearby Hollidaysburgh township. I decided to attend in order to look at their archive material.

The rest of the afternoon was spent on the pedestrian bridge at Altoona railroad station observing and photographing the many passenger and goods trains passing through Altoona on their transcontinental routes. I became aware of several schoolchildren making their way home across the footbridge, and pondered on the thought that my father would have made many such journeys along this route during his schooldays.

A sallow youth passed by and, upon seeing my camera, asked me if I wanted to take his picture. I shook my head and he walked on. His features seemed strangely familiar, but I could not fathom why this was so.

Then it was time for me to take a final walk from the station to the site of the butcher's shop. As I walked I imagined how my father, parents and siblings must have taken the very same route all those years ago. They would have gone this way to deliver the meat produce orders onto the train, collect goods and maybe go off to New York or Philadelphia. From here they would have gone to university and college. From here they would have gone away to war.

It was now time to take the short journey to Hollidaysburgh to meet the members of the Genealogical Society. I was introduced to their librarian, Cindy Rajala, who listened to my story with interest and then proceeded to search the city directories and archives for more information on Isadore J Schwartz. Cindy managed to find pre and post-war entries which confirmed my father residing at 1111 18th Street, first as a student and later as a radio technician with WVAM radio. Alas no picture of the butcher's shop could be located, but a promise was made to continue the search in the future.

She then posed a question to me: "What do you think your mother's reaction would have been to all the work you have done to discover your father's real name and learn about his background?"

At first I could not think of an answer to this. Then Cindy

thoughtfully provided me with one: "I think she would have been very proud of you taking the time and trouble to find out about your father".

Her personal opinion about his reaction to my arrival in the world was not so favourable. She felt that for him, it had been an unwanted burden. At that time all he had wanted in life was to achieve academic success and go on to greater achievements. I would not say it was pleasing to hear this verdict, but in essence it was the unbiased truth, and the truth hurts sometimes.

The next morning was a wet and gloomy one. It was time to leave Altoona behind and travel back to Bruce and Charol's home in Millersville PA. Altoona had not given up any of its many secrets, but at least I had a clearer picture of the kind of society and environment my father had grown up in. He had become something of a local celebrity, working as a disc jockey and engineer for local radio station WVAM.

Our route home to Millersville was planned to go through the State of Maryland. This gave us the opportunity to visit Antietam National Civil War Battlefield, which had long been an interest of mine and was a fitting conclusion to our little excursion. The last few days had been truly momentous.

I completed my third and final week with Bruce and Charol by making a visit to Washington DC. This was an interesting event which had more to do with gaining a further insight into American history than looking for further Schwartz links.

The Pentagon, Arlington military cemetery and house, Ford's Theatre Museum, White House, the Ellipse, the Capitol building and Union station – all these venues and more made for a pleasant tourist-style day spent in the company of Charol and Chad Thompson. Then it was back to South Wales to reflect on all that I had learnt and consider the next move in my quest to learn more about the life and times of my father.

Waiting for me on my return was an A4 letter from Beth Copp. She had promised to send me some pictures of the time she had spent with my father, and true to her word these had now arrived. They comprised six images taken outside their home in Tarzana, CA, and at his wedding to Shirley in Michigan. The quality was average, but at least they were in colour.

I had three main impressions. The neighbourhood in California was very pleasant; from the wedding my father had an expression which conveyed a sort of resigned contentment; and last, but my no means least, he never seemed to age!

I was pleased to receive these pictures, although they also effectively confirmed that my mother and I had indeed been "brushed under the carpet".

Now I took time to read the splendid yearbook the High School had presented to me. Inside was the copy of my father's last school report and details of his attendance at the Junior High. A cameo photograph was attached showing a youthful Isadore. The photograph seemed to show a distinct similarity with the face of the sallow youth who had passed me on the Altoona railroad station footbridge! The mind can play strange tricks at times.

CHAPTER SEVENTEEN

AMERICAN CITIZEN

Some time back in 2010, former 437th TCG radio operator Don Bolce had invited me to come to the group's annual association reunion. I told him I was really interested, but didn't commit myself. The attractions of attending were obvious. I would be able to meet Don, Tommie Thompson and others who had served with my father at Ramsbury. Somebody might just remember him.

I could also break my return journey in Detroit and meet up with LeAnn. This would afford me the opportunity of visiting the city of Ann Arbor, whose very name had held a mystical symbolism with me for many years.

On the other hand I asked myself whether, at a reunion of WWII veterans, I wouldn't perhaps be viewed as an outsider. How would they react to learning that I was Staff Sergeant Izzy Schwartz's son? I put off making the final decision.

After my return from Pennsylvania a "roster booklet" arrived through the mail. This very professional publication contained details of the 437th 2010 reunion in San Diego, California, urging everyone to "Go West" and attend the 2011 event in Portland, Oregon.

I still wavered. For the moment I had more important things

on my mind. I had to collate all the documents required to enable me to request an interview at the US Embassy in Grosvenor Square, London. Among the many documents were the birth and death certificates of both my mother and father and my father's military service certification, which had to be applied for from the NPRC. LeAnn had again been more than helpful here and had obtained a copy from the authorities in California. I was particularly anxious to obtain this document, if only to learn the underlying reason for my father's demise at 43 years of age.

The multiple causes of death listed only served to underline the debilitating effects of diabetes. Fortunately I had no advance signs of such an ailment myself.

Aunt Marian had sent me my father's birth certificate, which, after a lapse of 46 years, still had his surname misspelt! In addition to all this I had to provide an identification footprint of myself. This meant locating old school reports, employment history and certification and, of course, my past and current passports.

Once I had satisfied myself that sufficient material had been collated, I established contact with the Embassy. They gave me an appointment to attend at 10 o'clock on the morning of June 14th. It was a relief to be given a date and time.

I drove up on the day before the appointment. Staying overnight at a hotel in the West London Borough of Hanwell meant that my early morning journey into the centre of London would take, at most, one hour. As additional back-up I had researched several alternative inward routes should there be any unforeseen failure of the metro system. Come hell or high water, I was not going to be late for this appointment.

Awakening at 6 am, I prepared myself, took a hasty breakfast and then proceeded to make the 15-minute walk to Manor Park station. Already the sun was rising in the sky, with the weather set to continue its recent good run.

The indicator board advised customers that all inbound journeys were running to schedule, though, as my tube train pulled into the station, it was already full to near capacity with commuters travelling to their central London workplaces. Every weekday this early, uncomfortable, robotic ritual is pursued by thousands of people from different ethnic and educational backgrounds. On this particular morning I would be joining them secure in the knowledge that this particular journey was, a one off. If I ever had to do a similar journey in the future, it would be purely for leisure purposes!

After changing trains at Green Park I finally reached the nearest station to the Embassy, Bond Street. Alighting from the train, it was a walk of a few blocks before I caught my first sight of Grosvenor Square and, in one corner, the looming columned quadratic building that is the Embassy. By now the time had moved on to 9. 15, and I felt a slight sinking feeling as two substantial lines of people appeared. Back in 1977 I had practically walked straight into the building, but the world has changed a lot since then. I just had to be patient and trust that I would clear security in time to be permitted entry before 1000 hours.

Eventually, after the inevitable and necessary checks and searches, I was directed to the side of the building to a reception desk. The staff took my details and telephoned the Embassy official dealing with my application, advising him of my arrival. After being directed to the appointments waiting room, I waited for my name to be called. It was now 1000 hours precisely.

The room itself was fairly basic with rows of plastic seating and the inevitable automated snack machines in each corner. At one end of the room was a line of around eight separate glass-fronted counters. From time to time a number was called out and people then would go up to the relevant counter to process their respective applications and requests with a waiting official. I too had been given a number and told to await my turn.

Looking back on this day I had assumed, perhaps rather naively, that I would be interviewed in a private room on a face-to-face basis. With this in mind I had arrived attired in my best suit, shirt and tie and in shoes that were polished like a mirror.

Looking round the waiting room and comparing myself to the other people there I felt like a bank manager attending a meeting of recently-admitted immigrants! Very shortly I would be faced with standing and conversing with embassy officials through a little glass security barrier. Realistically I suppose one had to realise that this was not a bank serving customers but rather an embassy, where high security is a paramount consideration.

Finally at 10. 45 my number was called and I proceeded to the designated counter, to come face to face with the official I had spoken to by telephone some weeks before. This gentleman was both affable and extremely helpful and we carefully went through all my documentation page by page, picture by picture, until a complete portfolio of the relevant facts had been assembled. This was then taken away to be scrutinised and copied before being returned to me later.

In the meantime I had been assigned the task of compiling a factual account of how my mother and father had come to meet each other in London during that distant time in 1944. In my mind I already had several dates and possible social venues memorised, together with the exact location of my father's wartime air base in England. It was now simply a case of my compiling a plausible and reasonably factual account of the circumstances leading up to my conception. The official left me to write this down in my own time, and I sat down and began to compile my story.

The time was approaching midday as I indicated that my account was ready for inspection. After collecting this from the counter, the official informed me that another wait was in prospect before I would be interviewed by someone from the legal department. Then I would sign a formal declaration, pay a fee and await the return of my documents. Once again I sat down. This was one long day, and it was not yet over.

Finally my name was called and, upon returning to the hatch, I was given an assurance that all the documentation and photographs were in order and would be returned to me very shortly. The copies would now be sent to the US Department of State in Washington DC, where a decision would be made. This, I was informed, would take between six months and two years. I hoped I would live that long!

Once more I sat down, but this time I knew the day's proceedings were coming to an end. Sure enough, after a few minutes had passed by I was called for the final time. A female staff member passed my documents back through to me and, with a smile, exclaimed, "Mr Spencer – you were a war baby, weren't you!" I confirmed this with a smile.

Standing alongside her was the legal representative I had seen earlier. He leaned forward towards the glass and said, "Mr Spencer, I have read through your story and found it very interesting. I think that it would make a very good movie".

I was quite flattered by this remark and thanked the official, telling him I had an idea to try and write a book about everything that had transpired.

"Well, if you do write it then please come back again" he said. "We'd sure like to be able to read it. "

His reply was a very pleasant end to my visit and the contrast in attitude compared to my 1977 appearance could not have been more pronounced.

On my journey home that day, my mind constantly drifted back to the experience at the Embassy. I wondered what my chances of obtaining US citizenship really were. The interviewing official at the Embassy had expressed an optimistic viewpoint of my chances of success, but six months to two years waiting for such a decision seemed like an eternity to me and there was still the nagging doubt that someone in Washington would find an anomaly which would warrant refusal of my application.

There would only be one shot at this and I had just fired it. Now it would be time to concentrate on future upcoming events.

I had to make my mind up whether to attend the upcoming reunion in Portland, Oregon. I decided to telephone Neil Stevens, who had attended a previous 437th reunion at the same venue some 21 years previously. Neil told me he was sure the veterans would make me most welcome.

My mind was then finally made up, and I started to make enquiries for plane tickets to Portland in September. When planning my journey I included a stop-off in Detroit in the itinerary for the homebound section of my flight. This would enable me to visit Ann Arbor and Ypsilanti - two places which were firmly lodged in my psyche.

When I told LeAnn of my plans, she very kindly invited me to stay at her home and offered to drive me to Kalamazoo to meet my stepsister, Beth Copp. Maybe a face-to face meeting with Beth would prove to be productive in unlocking one or two vital new pieces of information on the life and times of Isadore Joseph Schwartz.

In addition to taking me to this rendezvous, LeAnn had promised to show me around Ann Arbor and the surrounding neighbourhood. She had labelled this forthcoming event the "IJS memorial tour".

On September 20th I began my journey to Portland. I flew out two days earlier than necessary in order not to be jet-lagged when the actual reunion began. My transatlantic flight took me first to Boston, Massachusetts, where I connected with an ongoing flight to Portland. Finally, after landing in the late evening, I made my way via tramway to the Embassy Suites hotel in the downtown area. The journey, with all the connecting links involved, was seamless. My early arrival meant that I had plenty of time, using the excellent tramway system, to explore the city and surrounding areas.

On the second day, after returning from one of these explorations, I observed that a notice had appeared in the hotel foyer requesting all members of the 437th Troop Carrier Group Association to report to the Presidential Suite on the 11th floor at 1630 hours in order to complete registration. All very ship-shape and military fashion – as one would expect.

While reading this instruction I noticed in front of me two gentlemen smartly attired in summer clothing. Both were wearing light-coloured polo shirts which bore the inscription "437th TC Gp". The expression on their faces was one of deep concentration.

I hurried past them to the elevator. In less than an hour I would be meeting them face to face. The thought of it was slightly unnerving. Finally I left my room and made my way along the corridor to the Presidential Suite.

All my apprehension melted away within a few seconds of entering the room. Small groups of people were quietly conversing; others were registering at a desk. Light refreshments were laid out on a large table.

I quickly introduced myself to the welcoming committee. Recognising Don Bolce from his internet images, I went over and introduced myself to him. He presented me to his wife, Bonnie. The whole atmosphere was convivial, with everyone being extremely friendly. My one disappointment was the news that Tommie Thompson had fallen ill and could not attend. That was a real pity. When I had spoken to him the previous month and told him how much I was looking forward to meeting him at the reunion, he had still been intent on coming.

But for Tommie's skills in ditching the "Terror of the Ozarks", which had run out of fuel after taking off from the airfield at the base of the Rock of Gibraltar en route to Ramsbury on August 23rd 1944, the crew and all its passengers would have drowned in the icy waters off the Cornish coast at Land's End. My father would, of course, have been among the fatalities, and I would never have existed. Instead, everyone had been rescued by two British minesweepers (HMS *Willow* and HMS *Sycamore*) and returned safe and sound to dry land at St Ives.

During the summer of 2010 I established contact with Lynn Gregory, the stepdaughter of Rollo Jacobs, the plane's navigator. Her father had, she said, written an extensive eye-witness account of the incident. She sent it, along with other memorabilia, to the hotel for me and those at the reunion to read. As the package was addressed to me, I was the first to read this fascinating account of what must have been a terrifying incident.

When carrying out his duties as the crew's radio operator, my father had been responsible for transmitting the SOS message prior to the ditching of the craft into the sea. The plane stayed afloat, even after one engine had been torn off in the impact. One mention of my father during these moments of drama read: "We checked and found everyone was all right. Schwartz was complaining that he had hurt his back and he was afraid that we were all going to die out there. But, as we found out later, he was a chronic complainer and wasn't really hurt at all!"

Rollo's account continued to describe the drama that unfolded, and it was fascinating to read. The ditching had not been without additional terror for my father, as one of the two small life-rafts had failed to inflate properly. It had drifted away from the plane shortly after the crew and its passengers had evacuated. Altogether they numbered eight men. The priority was to get away from the plane as quickly as possible to avoid being dragged down should it sink. Although it was August the sea was rough and cold.

The remaining life-raft had inflated correctly, but was only intended for four people and now had too many occupants. They were some distance from the shoreline and there was a real danger of it filling with water. Consequently, because my father was the heaviest, he and three other men had to leave the raft and get into the water. They then had to hang on until the rescue ships arrived. Altogether this took some 40-45 minutes, though it must have seemed an eternity.

Before the ships arrived, after half an hour or so, the tail of the plane began to rise in the air. It kept rising until the plane was in a vertical position. Then it slid into the water and disappeared. Fortunately the life raft was by now a sufficient distance away to be safe from the resulting suction.

After the eventual rescue the two ships had taken the men to St Ives, where they had disembarked onto one of the ship's lifeboats. A Catholic priest had waded out to greet their arrival, watched from the shore by what seemed to be the entire population of St Ives who had turned out to welcome them! Many years later, the pilot, Tommie Thompson, returned to England and met the freighter captain who had rescued them way back in August 1944.

When I read this account it made me think that on that particular day, it was not the time for the occupants of the "Terror of the Ozarks " to die. As my father had expressed in his "St Louis letter", fate is very unpredictable at times

The two serious-looking gentlemen I had noticed in the foyer turned out to be Tom Kilker, the head of the family hosting this reunion, and Paul Proulx, the secretary of the 437th TCG Association. No wonder they had been looking so serious. The success or failure of the reunion lay in their hands. Now the frowns had been replaced by smiles! Everything was going to plan. Their efforts would be rewarded many times in the coming days.

Then I recognised another face, that of Vic Affatigato, a former member of the 85th squadron, my father's unit. In 2010 Vic had sent me an email: "Hello! I was not aware that Izzy Schwartz had a son. Your father was a very likeable guy. He flew in all the major battles of Europe. He was forced to ditch in the Channel during one of them. I can remember his acquiring an English accent. He used this on his radio program. He came to two or three of our reunions. "

I introduced myself. "So you are Izzy's son," he said. "Do you follow the Jewish faith?"

"No, I don't," I told him.

"Did Izzy look after you when the war ended?"

For a moment the answer stuck in my throat. How I wished

it could have been different. I told Vic the truth, and he made no comment.

He went on to talk about his life and times. His family had emigrated from Sicily when he was three and still went back there for family holidays. He vividly described life in Sicily and the strong sense of community prevailing there. I could see a lot of parallels with my own adopted country of Wales, where a similar community spirit still survives, even if it has been diluted somewhat by the more materialistic nature of modern society.

I asked Vic how frequently airmen visited London when they were at Ramsbury and whether he had ever accompanied my father on such a visit. Unfortunately, he said, the fact that each of them had leave at different times had meant that this was impossible.

Later I got into conversation with Tom Kilker. He told me that he had been a glider pilot and had landed his glider on the Cherbourg peninsula during the early hours of D-Day, having been transported there from Ramsbury by a C-47 Dakota aircraft of the 437th. His vivid memories of the hair-raising events of that historic morning held me spellbound.

"Tom", I asked, "did you know my father, radio operator Isadore Schwartz?"

"Of course I knew your dad" he replied. "He was the biggest guy on the base!"

His answer was both amusing and heart-warming. It felt good to be in the presence of someone who had not only played a part in D-Day but had known and still remembered my father.

I spent the next few days in the pleasant company of the men of the 437th and their families. I felt completely accepted. We toured the wine-growing region of the Willamette valley, took a steamship ride on the Columbia river and - a fitting climax – flew, courtesy of the local flying club, in a glider with dual controls.

That really was something. We left the hotel early on Sunday morning in a convoy of cars, heading for the glider field. The weather that morning was mildly inclement – light rain with a prevailing westerly wind. We all hoped it would clear up within the hour. It was still unchanged when we arrived, but fortunately a canopy sheltered us from the worst effects. Coffee, sandwiches and hot soup had been laid on by the club and there was a warm, determined feeling that, come what may, we were all going to enjoy both the visit and experience.

My abiding image from this adventure is of 437th radio operator Lewis Shank being manually hoisted out of his wheelchair into a glider cockpit. No way was he going to miss out on this experience. His determination embodied the spirit of the war years.

As I stood observing these proceedings, I suddenly became aware of someone in close proximity to me. It was Vic Affatigato. Looking up at the sky, which had by now lost its earlier cover of grey cloud and drizzle he quietly made the following observation: "What a good thing that the weather has finally cleared up so we can fly".

After a few more minutes of deep thought he continued, "The United States is truly the greatest country in the world. If you're prepared to work hard, and keep working hard, then the sky is the limit to what you can achieve".

I listened to this statement from someone who had clearly become a great patriot of his adopted country. These sentiments had some parallels with my own feelings towards my adopted country, Wales, though, due to the size of the economy, the horizons are somewhat lower.

When all the veterans, and some of their wives, had completed their flights, it was my turn to take to the air. Assisted by some members of the flying club I climbed into the tiny two-seater cockpit and my instructor co-pilot joined me. He indicated where my feet should be positioned in relation to the pedal controls.

Then the Perspex cover of the cockpit was closed and the light aircraft to which we were attached edged slowly forward. Tow wire tension between the glider and the power aircraft was established and we started to move along the grass runway. Acceleration along the bumpy surface was rapid, and in a matter of moments we achieved lift-off and rose up steeply, clearing the field and surrounding countryside.

The next forty-five minutes were an amazing experience. Many varying vistas to the left, right, below and above flashed by as we circled around, gaining height as we did so. Once a suitable altitude had been achieved, my instructor communicated with the power aircraft and simultaneously operated a lever which mechanically released our tow wire from it. We were now completely under the influence of the prevailing winds and air currents. Nature was, in effect, our source of power, our means of survival.

The whole of this time we were in radio communication with ground control, both giving and receiving constant updates on our exact location and flight conditions. This and the whistling of the wind were the only sounds. Above me on the right-hand side I could see another glider which had taken off from the same runway a few minutes earlier.

The highlight of the flight came when the instructor sitting behind allowed me to take control of the glider for a few minutes. Then, as we circled high above the Oregon landscape, he announced: "I am now going to demonstrate to you what happens when a glider gets into a stall situation". The next few seconds that followed were dramatic as we started to nosedive and I realised that the man behind me really did have my life (and his) in his hands.

Quickly (thank goodness) control was regained and contact made with ground control to establish permission to prepare for landing. Soon we were descending and positioning the glider for touchdown and the eventual bumpy, decelerating ride along the surface of the grassy field before coming to a final halt. My flight was indeed a memorable experience and made me appreciate what great skill and nerve the D-Day pilots must have had. Back then they did not have the facility of a designated landing strip, full daylight and good weather. If that was not enough to make a landing difficult there was also a "welcoming committee" awaiting them in the form of the German military.

With the glider flights completed it was then time to return to our hotel in Portland and prepare for the evenings banquet.

That evening was to be the highlight of the reunion. It was a grand occasion, held in the hotel main function room with, as one might expect, a photocall, a formal opening dedication, singing of the national anthem and the first airing of a new song penned by the son of a veteran, Colorado schoolteacher Bob Campbell. Bob's song was very funny and innovative. It even included a line, written in my honour, mentioning the UK. He had written the lyrics on the notice board alongside the rostrum:

Now we're friends and family across the USA
And we're all included, no matter what you say
From New York to Oregon (and even the UK)
We can get some hospitality
(and we don't have to pay).

Considering that there had been no rehearsal, the rendition of the song by the assembled diners was quite astonishing! It was assisted by Bob's excellent playing of a ukulele and the dulcet tones of our lead singers Tom Kilker and Tony Affatigato.

Following the meal, secretary Paul Proulx made a speech in which he gave a resume of all the events of the past year, including calling for a momentary pause of silence for everyone to pay their respects in memory of the veterans who had passed away during that time. He then went on to mention how he had "received a call from Wales back in March from Norm Spencer" and was very pleased that I had travelled to attend the 39th reunion of the 437th TGC association. " He then invited me to come up to the rostrum, take the microphone and say a few words. I had already requested this privilege.

My lack of experience in public speaking restricted my speech to just a few words to say thank you to the veterans for their past actions in securing the freedom of Europe and expressing my pride at being the son of 437th radio operator Isadore Joseph Schwartz. I was warmly applauded off the rostrum. I wonder what my father would have made of that? After a gap of some 48 years the son of a Schwartz was once more making his presence felt at a military reunion.

Now it was time to say goodbye to all the people I had met, especially the veterans, and express my hopes that I would be able to see them again at the 2012 reunion in Charleston, South Carolina.

Don Bolce and his wife Bonnie came up to me and said they were sure that my father would have been very proud of me. I felt humbled by their observations. I said goodbye to several other people, and one farewell in particular will stay in my memory forever. When I came to shake hands with Vic

Affatigato and his son Tony, Vic said in his unmistakeable Brooklyn accent: "Izzy was a good guy".

With that Vic turned smartly on his heels and walked away. Sadly he was to pass away six months later, and another link with my father was broken.

My time in Portland was spent in the presence of America's "greatest generation", and we shall never see their like again. If I could sum up the whole experience, I think it could be defined by a brief off-the-cuff remark from one of the veterans' sons, Lee Ferguson: "We are all family here".

In the early hours of September 26th I left Portland and flew to Minneapolis, where I took a connecting flight to Detroit. There LeAnn was waiting there to greet me. En route to her home in Ann Arbor she took a minor diversion through Ypsilanti to the exact place where the temporary university student accommodation called West Lodge had stood. Before this became a facility for the students of the University of Michigan, it had been vacant land adjacent to the enormous Willow Run Ford Motor Company manufacturing complex. Now it was a private residential area with broad level streets and neat suburban housing.

I alighted from the car for a brief photo shoot. Although the landscape had changed since my father's time there, I felt a real sense of connection. It was, after all, the place where he had received my mother's letters, including the one which told him he had become a father for the first time in his life.

It's worth recalling his response: "Needless to say your news was most revealing and very surprising. After reading your first letter I was stunned and it took me several days to regain my composure. It doesn't make sense and when your second letter arrived it renewed my perplexity. I'm really at a loss as far as doing anything is concerned. "

For a few minutes I thought of these words that my father had written from his student accommodation near the very spot where I was now standing. In this neighbourhood, my father had opened those fateful letters, read the contents and entered a temporary state of mental turmoil. I wondered how his family back in Altoona would have reacted if they had known of his new-found status of father. The School of Engineering had a very demanding curriculum which had no place for anyone experiencing this kind of dilemma and the possible anxiety at having to tell his parents.

These brief moments of reflection over, I stepped back into LeAnn's car and we sped off to home to Ann Arbor. The following morning LeAnn took me into the city centre to the location of another address with an emotional significance: 703 Church Street, the address on the back of my father's wartime photo.

Once more I alighted from the car for another photoshoot, and using the time delay feature I took a shot of myself in the porch of the three-storey property with the front door in the background. It was strange to see this image and imagine my father standing there some sixty-five years before.

On this early October morning the centre of Ann Arbor was a hive of activity. Groups of neatly-dressed students - many of the male students were wearing ties - were hurrying purposefully between lectures and seminars. What, I wondered, were their hopes and aspirations? As I watched them, I thought of the thousands of young ex-GIs like my father who at the end of the war had taken full advantage of the GI Bill of Rights and descended upon Ann Arbor.

Judging by the monochrome pictures I had seen, the atmosphere and optimism among students at that time would have been euphoric, and my father would have been in the middle of all this euphoria. Many of this new influx would have been conscripted into the armed forces straight after leaving high school. Instead of going to university, they had had to endure the manifold horrors and ordeals of war. Now this was their one great chance to catch up on those missed years, to lay the sound foundations of their professional future.

The survivors of the great conflict were the lucky ones. If they were prepared to make the necessary sacrifices and concentrate fully on their studies, then the chance of achieving the "American Dream" would be high.

We paid a brief visit to the imposing, ivy-covered building with shining floors and ceramic tiling which was the School of Engineering. The building was the very same one where my father would have undertaken his studies.

After inspecting the educational and recreation facilities LeAnn pointed out something unusual outside the main entrance. A circular brass medallion was embedded in the second tier of the stone steps. Next to it a wall plaque bore the following inscription:

Here at 2. 00 am on October 14th 1960, John Fitzgerald Kennedy first defined the Peace Corps. He stood at the place marked by the medallion and was cheered by a large and enthusiastic student audience for the hope and promise his idea gave the world.

I stood on the steps and got LeAnn to take my photo at this historical spot. With the photo-shoot over, we headed to Kalamazoo and the arranged meeting with my stepsister, Beth

Copp. Our drive took us through the flat landscapes and sprawling freeways of Southern Michigan state to the outskirts of Kalamazoo. The name comes from a Potowatomi word and is often a source of amusement, but I was not here for amusement. Instead my mission was to meet up with someone who, up to now, had been just an image on a photograph, a voice on the telephone.

As LeAnn had felt it would be wise to meet on neutral ground, I had mutually agreed a suitable rendezvous at an out-of town restaurant. We met up with Beth and her husband Gary in a branch of the Bob Evans restaurant chain. To my disappointment, she had little to add to what had she had already told me about my father and had none of his personal effects. She could tell me that after leaving Altoona for Los Angeles in 1959, he had worked for the Lockheed Corporation, a major aeronautical manufacturer both then and now.

He had also worked for RCA, and for a time he had, she said, been self-employed and run a sound-recording business. But during these years he had suffered from diabetes and his illness had slowly but surely affected his ability to work. Days off became weeks off, and eventually he had to give up work completely.

I thanked Beth for this brief insight into the closing years of my father's life and we said farewell and left Kalamazoo in the pouring rain. The following day we took time to visit the Bentley Historical Library, the building where, in the previous year, LeAnn had made that momentous discovery.

For breakfast we made use of an all-day diner in nearby Ypsilanti. This establishment had been around for many years and sepia and monochrome pictures of WWII aircraft and crews were hanging on every interior wall. I looked to see if my father was portrayed; he wasn't, but as he had lived nearby as a student, it was highly likely that he would have dined there.

My brief time in Michigan was almost over, and although not overly productive in terms of information, it had been a historic experience. My "IJS memorial tour" was completed, and on Thursday October 4th I said my farewells to LeAnn and flew home.

I still had things to do. Earlier in the year I had contacted Henry C Weinberg, an Altoona resident. Unfortunately he had been away on vacation when I was there. An influential member of the Jewish community in the city, he had unearthed for me a photo, taken in the 1950s, of my grandparents standing in front of their kosher butcher's shop.

I telephoned him to see if he had anything further to add. Did he have any memories of my father? All he could tell me was that as a teenager he used to "hang out" on the street corner with Isadore and that my father had a beautiful voice with which he used to recite the works of William Shakespeare.

During the first week of December 2011, I received a call from the US Embassy in London confirming that my application for citizenship had been approved in Washington DC and that my passport would be sent to me in approximately three weeks' time.

My new US passport means a lot to me. I might only use it for ease of transit when travelling to the US, but it is tangible proof that a vital part of my identity has been officially recognised.

In effect I am English by birth, American by right and Welsh by residence – an unusual identity.

Now, with my US citizenship confirmed, I fondly imagined that my great voyage of discovery was over. I was wrong.

Shortly before Christmas I contacted Philip Marguish, a man who had grown up in Altoona during the 60s and attended the same high school as my father. An expert on the history of local broadcasting in the area, he provided me with some details on the radio station WVAM, where my father had worked. He also gave me the name of veteran broadcaster Dick DeAndrea.

I emailed Dick to ask if he knew anything about my father's time at WVAM. His reply was very helpful:

Norman, I had the opportunity to check into Mr Schwartz, he was actually more an engineer than an announcer, and as far as I can recall, along with some old friends, more involved with WKMC Roaring Spring rather than with WVAM. He wanted to play classical and the station owner (William Ketner) wasn't too interested in that. He wanted more a contemporary sound.

Mr Schwartz was very interested in broadcasting but never seemed to make an impact while Ketner was there.

I will always appreciate Dick DeAndrea providing me with this brief but interesting insight into the character and unfulfilled ambition of my father.

Knowing that my father had communicated with a wide audience left me with a slightly envious feeling. It was a strange kind of emotion to experience. Here was someone known to thousands, yet seemingly unwilling to be known to his own flesh and blood.

I would give anything to have been one of his listeners and to write into the station with a record request. It really would have been something to have had my father read out this request live on air. I imagine him stopping mid-sentence. Perhaps he would have had to go off-microphone in a state of shock! But of course, that's just a dream.

CHAPTER EIGHTEEN

CLOSURE

2012 had begun quietly, but activity would build slowly as the year progressed. Just before Christmas I had an pleasant surprise. Cousin Scott had located another 78 rpm 90-second disc made by my father during his military training in the US. He had made this recording to send to his sister Ruth, and told her briefly about the situation "back home".

I received the record from Scott by post. After checking that there was no damage, I had carefully repacked it and forwarded it to David Grant in York, England. David in turn had duly copied the recorded material onto a CD disc and safely returned it to me.

There was not quite the same impact on hearing this second recording. Nevertheless it had a magnetic quality and poignancy. During the message he mentioned that he was "enjoying good health". Although this was simply a casual remark, there was a sad irony about it.

On my original visit to Ramsbury and the tour of the airfield, Roger Day had suggested returning to discover more. He had suggested going in early springtime, when the undergrowth would still be dormant. This would make things much easier when it came to identifying sites of past buildings or even uncovering "souvenirs" of the past.

We arranged a meeting for the 21st February at 10.30 am. This time I had a lot more knowledge of the significance of what had happened there during WWII, and indeed of my father's part in it. Once more we walked the lanes and fields around this once-expansive complex. Exploring the undergrowth adjacent to where the 437th's nissen huts would have been, we discovered some discarded glass bottles. I wondered if my own father had been responsible for such littering!

Roger took me to the exact location where the radio operators would have had their headquarters and nearby residential huts, now an open field in a natural hollow. I could not resist the temptation to ask Roger to take my photograph standing at this spot. As the shutter button was pressed he said to me, "I'm sure your father is looking down on you right now and is very pleased that you are here".

We continued our tour, inspecting the remains of what had been an air raid shelter, passing by the site of the former officers' quarters and other outbuildings, and of course the site where the chow huts would have been! Now all that remained of the place where the men of the 437th would have enjoyed sustenance and camaraderie was a ploughed field.

We then drove to the nearby village of Axford and enjoyed a light meal at the Red Lion Hotel. Roger's idea of directing me there was not entirely inspired by hunger. In the adjacent car park was a large memorial stone. The inscription on it was dedicated to the members of the 437th Troop Carrier Group, stationed at Ramsbury during WWII. Halfway down the stone was a reference to something that had happened in the vicinity.

On March 11th 1944, a Douglas Dakota C-47 had crashed during training operations. Major Donald E. Bradley and 1st Lt Gaylord Strong had lost their lives as a result. It seemed that such manoeuvres in a friendly location were not without risk, and my father would also have been exposed to such hazards. It was thoughtful of Roger to take me to this spot. I also learned that Neil Stevens had been instrumental in having the memorial placed there.

The afternoon was rounded off with a visit to Littlecote Manor and gardens. This place had been used as a command post for the US and British forces prior to D-Day – a virtual hive of activity.

If the gardens were impressive, then the interior of this building was even more so. Roger explained how the military had utilised the rooms back then for work and leisure purposes. There was an active museum in one of the rooms, displaying artefacts from that era. Roger had been involved in collecting and setting up this historical facility.

At the end of a beautiful sunny day, I bade my host farewell and headed home to South Wales. The "Roster Booklet" with details and pictures of the 437th's 2011 Portland reunion arrived through the post shortly afterwards. I was pleased, even a little flattered, to see myself featured in several of the pictures, and aware that the next reunion, in Charleston SC, would be the very last one. I decided to attend, and to extend my time in the US by going to see the Thompsons again on the way home.

Remembering how St Louis journalist Susan Weich had originally helped out by posting details of my search, I decided to contact her with the news of my successes. She replied, congratulating me on the outcome and wanting to know fuller details, so that she could update her readers on the story. A series of email exchanges followed during which the details of my story were further defined, along with the transmission of a photograph of my father's graduation photograph and one of myself, aged 10, wearing a Davy Crockett raccoon hat.

In order to gauge my reaction to all these discoveries more accurately, she asked me to make a telephone call to her at the newspaper. I duly did this and a brief conversation ensued during which I did my best to answer her questions truthfully and accurately.

On the 20th June Susan posted an article on the *St Louis Post-Dispatch* website. The two photographs I had sent her were posted side by side at the top. Alongside was a heading which read: "War baby whose father had St Louis connection finally gets answers". This was neither true or untrue, as even to the present day I have not been able to determine if my father really was in St Louis when he typed the apparently final letter to my mother.

The article under the heading continued:

Norman Spencer of Wales knew nothing about his father until his mother Doris died in 1976 and he found letters that detailed an affair with a US Army airman named Joseph Schwartz.

The notes talked about Schwartz's studies at a school in Michigan where he said he hoped to get a government radio operator's license and return to England. But in the last letter, Schwartz said that a woman named Mary, the sister of an old friend, had come to visit, and he had gotten her pregnant. They married, he said, and he was living in St. Louis, learning his father-in-law's business.

In the final paragraph, Schwartz said to tell Norman 'some story of his father's death during the war or another story equally acceptable when he's old enough to understand". He encouraged Spencer's mother to forget him and marry an Englishman.

But she never married, Spencer said, and she moved from job to job as a cook and a housekeeper. Spencer, now 66, contacted the Post-Dispatch three years ago for help in locating Schwartz when the paper was working on a story about war babies.

Spencer also contacted the National Personnel Records Center in Overland. Workers there identified more than 130 Joseph Schwartzes from World War II, but Spencer didn't know his father's middle initial, hometown or exact date of birth.

Spencer contacted me last week with the end of the story.

After his St Louis leads did not pan out, Spencer placed an ad in the Ann Arbor (Mich.) News with his father's photograph.

He got one reply, from an Ann Arbor resident, a woman who agreed to help him. She searched for the student records at the University of Michigan and found that an Isadore Joseph Schwartz had attended there, and his home address was in Altoona, Pa.

A high school in Altoona found Schwartz's records and mailed Spencer a photo, but they said Schwartz had died on Feb 3, 1966.

The picture, however, was a close match to the WWII photograph, Spencer said.

A library search located a family tree and a potential aunt, Marian Garfinkel of Philadelphia. Spencer called and asked if she knew a WWII soldier named Isadore Joseph Schwartz. She replied "He was my brother".

Spencer didn't reveal the true reason for the call but instead wrote a long letter of explanation. Two weeks later, Garfinkel called Spencer and said she accepted his story even though she had no idea of his existence, he said. She also contacted her sister, Ruth Johns, in California.

In May 2010, Spencer visited Johns, and she gave him directions to the cemetery where his father was buried. Spencer took the train to San Fernando and walked the two miles from the station to the cemetery.

It took more than 30 minutes of searching, but Spencer finally found the horizontal headstone with Hebrew lettering and the inscription: 'Isadore Joseph Schwartz, 1922-1966, beloved husband, son and brother'.

"What impacted me immediately was the missing word – father,"
he said. "My next reaction upon seeing the Hebrew inscriptions was the
underlining of my Jewish heritage - for years I had focused entirely on
the American aspect".

Standing at the grave, Spencer said he slowly realised that after 34
years of searching, he had finally located his father. He placed a framed
picture of himself and his mother together with the message that said:
"For the freedom of Europe, thank you. Your loving son, Norman."

Spencer found out that his dad was employed at the time of his
death as an electrical technician, which was Spencer's occupation too. He
also learned from some military buddies that his father was a personable
man and a born entertainer.

"The letter I found which indicated that he was living in St Louis
circa 1947 may well have been true but other contents were not... I
was his only child," Spencer said.

He said he will always be disappointed in his father's deception,
but that's in the past.

"It's not a happy, Hollywood-style ending, but at last I now know
a great deal more about what was the missing half of my identity",
Spencer said.

When I read Susan's professionally-written article I felt a glow
of satisfaction from such an accolade.

The article did contain one slight inaccuracy – I had
mistakenly told Susan there were more than 130 Joseph
Schwartzes from World War II, but the correct number was 125.

The summer of 2012 brought no further revelations, which
was no surprise. September soon came around and with it the
time to travel to Charleston SC for the final 437th reunion - "the
last hurrah". I would be travelling with less apprehension than
the previous year, but also with a little sadness. News had come

through to me via Neil Stevens that "Tommie" Thompson would not be attending the reunion. Apparently his health had taken a setback and this meant he would be unable to travel.

This was a real disappointment. I had spoken to Tommie at the turn of the year and he had been enthusiastic about going to Charleston. Now I would not get to meet the man whose piloting skills in 1944 had saved his crew, including my father, from a watery grave.

In life you cannot have everything you would wish for, so I travelled in the anticipation of seeing other members of the 437th and their families. There was also the prospect of seeing something of historic Charleston itself.

My flight to Charleston would involve a connecting flight in Philadelphia and I would arrive at my destination in the early evening. At Philadelphia airport I would be entering the United States as a citizen of that country for the very first time.

When I entered the immigration hall, it was packed with passengers from the incoming international flights. I joined one of the queues for US citizens and soon it was my turn to approach the passport desk. Proudly handing the official my passport, I awaited the all-clear to proceed through.

As the man in uniform pensively thumbed through the unused pages of my new documentation, slight doubts began to enter my mind. Supposing, just supposing, there was something wrong with my passport – maybe the Embassy in London had not finalised something, maybe the authorities had not activated it, maybe…

My thoughts were interrupted as the controller closed the pages, asked the usual security and customs questions and handed the passport back to me. Relief! But then the controller held his hand out and said, "OK Mr Spencer, that seems fine, but you cannot enter the United States until you provide me with the correct answer to this question. Yesterday, before you began to travel, something very important happened. It was not on the television, or in the newspapers, and not that many people knew about it - what happened? Unless you answer correctly, entry is forbidden."

Oh my! Was this a test of my citizenship, a measure of my knowledge of US constitution? Thinking quickly, I offered that perhaps a covert revolution had occurred somewhere in the past few hours which had affected the Western world.

"No! Have another try," said the official.

"There has been a catastrophic explosion at a nuclear power plant which is potentially life threatening but needs to be kept quiet until measures can be taken to counteract the radiation?"

Another shaking of the head. Now I really had run out of ideas. Seeing my dilemma, the controller leaned slightly forward.

"You really don't know? OK, yesterday was your birthday. That was a really important event, wasn't it? Now on your way - and enjoy your visit. Thank you."

What a relief! It proved that immigration officials really do have a sense of humour - even if it involves a heart-stopping moment for the person being questioned!

As sometimes happens, the best-laid plans can go wrong, and in this instance they did. My connecting flight took off late from Philadelphia. Looking out of my cabin window, I could see the bright lights of the city below. They did not however disappear, and we appeared to be on a circular route. Then came the announcement that one of the doors had a mechanical fault and we would have to return to 'Philly' for repairs. A replacement aircraft was found and we reloaded and took off. The end result was an arrival in Charleston well after midnight, when all public transport had ceased operation. Fortunately a kind stranger gave me a lift to my hotel.

It was good to meet up with some familiar faces at the Embassy Suites hotel on the outskirts of the city. The group had made the usual block booking, and a hospitality room was laid on for socialising.

Among the events planned was a visit to the local military base. We all gathered round an original WWII C-47 Dakota for a photocall. For the veterans who had served on board such an aircraft, it was a special moment. For myself, it was an appreciation of the dimensions of such a plane. I tried to visualise what a squadron of these machines would have looked and sounded like during those far-off days of conflict.

After visiting a modern-day hangar at the base and inspecting a modern troop carrier plane, it was time for a light lunch. Then there was a visit to the lecture theatre, where the attending veterans were invited up onto the stage to render their personal recollections from WWII.

The four days of the reunion seemed to speed by much more quickly than those in Portland. The banquet on the last evening was a grand affair. The evening began with a parade by the present-day military in honour of the veterans. Several speeches were made and an enjoyable meal served up. This really was the last great gathering of these people who had known each other for so many years and forged such great friendships. All good things have to come to an end eventually.

After saying my goodbyes on the final morning, I made my way to Charleston Airport. While sitting in the departure lounge, I caught sight of one of the veterans wheeling his hand luggage along to the departure gate. I had first met former power and glider pilot Bill Cheolas at the Portland reunion, and he was quite a character. Put another way, he would not be the type of person you would ever invite to undertake a sponsored silence! Now he was disappearing into the distance, having enjoyed the last-ever reunion with his 437th buddies. I hoped that he would look back with pleasure on past get-togethers and not be too morose about the inevitable ending.

My flight from Charleston took me back to Philadelphia, where I would meet up again with Bruce and Charol Thompson. The next two weeks would include a reunion with Aunt Marian at her flat, along with other tours and visits. Included in the itinerary was a return to the mountain city whose name was indelibly imprinted on my mind – Altoona PA.

The journey out to Altoona did not carry the same resonance as it had in the previous year, but there was some unfinished business to attend to. Shortly after the article written by Susan Weich for the *St Louis Post-Despatch* had been posted on line, I had received a response, by email, from a journalist working for the *Altoona Mirror*. Her name was Kay Stevens, and she had been directed towards the article by a relative living in Pittsburg. Now Kay was interested in my story, and she promised to research the archives of her newspaper to see if she could find any further information on my father.

Sure enough, after a couple of weeks, Kay kindly sent me some photocopies of various newspaper clippings which featured not only brief items about my father but some on other members of the Schwartz family. I had seen one or two of them before during my archives.com search, but many were new to me. One in particular caught my attention. Its headline, in bold type, read, "In Heavy Action". It read thus:

An Altoonan, S/Sgt Isadore J. Schwartz, a son of Mr and Mrs P. Schwartz of 1111 Eighteenth Street, was in the big D-Day invasion drive into France and a letter telling of the big undertaking was received in Altoona in time for Father's Day. Sgt Schwartz also included in the mail a copy of the Stars and Stripes dated June 7, which detailed the big drive across the Channel, also containing a picture of the convoy of ships. The paper was the most interesting one prized by the parents. "The biggest yet" is the way the soldier described the action on June 6. Sgt Schwartz entered the services two years ago and trained at Sedalia, Mo., and at Sioux Falls, S.D. He was home on a furlough in October, 1943. He was advanced rapidly in the ranks after receiving his wings. He has had many hours of flying. He was serving with the 85th squadron, 437th TCG before his overseas assignment. His many home friends know the sergeant as "Yossie". A brother, Leonard H Schwartz, is a second lieutenant in the armed forces.

I noted the reference to Father's Day. Sixteen months after D-Day, S/Sgt Isadore J. Schwartz would himself become a father. I wondered what he would have thought about when Father's Day came around. Had he looked around to see other families celebrating this annual event and perhaps felt the pain of regret? Or did he simply lock away any feelings that he might have had and carry on regardless?

Maybe sometimes he did think about his brief but affectionate wartime romance, the warm-hearted, generous woman he had left behind across the ocean in another country – and the son he had never met, who might have many of his own attributes. These are question I will never have answers to.

In her email and telephone communications with me, Kay Stevens had expressed a wish to publish an article about my story. Now I was travelling with the Thompsons and we were fast approaching the outskirts of Altoona. I called the *Altoona Mirror* office and arranged to meet Kay on our arrival in town.

We left the freeway and made our way there. Parking up

outside a very impressive set of premises, we made our way to the main entrance. We went to the main reception desk and introduced ourselves, and after signing in we were directed to the upstairs floor.

Kay was there at the top of the stairs to greet and take us to a conference room. We spent a pleasant half hour in discussion, with a photo-call, and left the building en route to our hotel accommodation. After checking in and finding our rooms, we prepared to move on for our first Altoona excursion. My previous calculations as to the exact location of the Schwartz's butcher's shop had turned out to be not strictly accurate. Google Earth locations are not as precise as I thought, but fortunately Aunt Marian had given me a more accurate description of the shop's location.

Forr's service station now stood on the exact spot, and the owners were interested to know about the reason for our visit there. Mr Forr and his wife had some memories of Leonard, my father's brother, and produced a couple of photographs showing the apex of Leonard's house in the background. One of the service station customers also had recollections of this "larger than life character", but alas, could not recall my father. Equally disappointing was the fact that no picture of the butcher's shop could be found, but at least I now knew exactly where it had once stood - which meant another photo opportunity featuring myself standing on the forecourt right where my grandparents would have toiled all those years ago.

The only image I had was one that had been sent to me in 2011 by Henry C Weinberg of the Greater Altoona Jewish Federation. It was a black-and-white picture showing my grandparents, in white aprons, standing in front of their premises. It was of newsprint quality, which meant a distinct lack of definition. Nevertheless a part of the shop window was visible and the words "meat market" could be identified.

This was the area of Altoona classified as the "5th Ward". The railroad museum had displayed a poster illustrating the ward and mentioned that it had another colloquial name - "Jew Hill". I thought it would be very appropriate to walk up the steep hill behind the service station, one which my father would surely have walked up many times.

I began the walk, occasionally turning around to photograph the view behind me. At last I reached the summit. It was a steep hill, though by South Wales standards it would only be moderate. Down below me the lay the streets of Altoona, with the hills and trees beyond the city lit up by the autumn evening sunshine. From my vantage point I could see the close proximity of the synagogue to the spot where the butcher's shop would have been. It was absorbing to think that in front of me was a landscape that would have played a formative part in my father's early life.

The similarity between what now lay before me and a typical South Wales panorama was uncanny. I cast my eye over the many steeply-sloping streets with row after row of housing. On the lower plateau lay an eclectic mixture of late 19th and early 20th century commercial and religious buildings, interspersed with more recent additions. Their presence provided evidence of a former era of industrial activity and achievement. It was almost as if I had been here decades before and had become an actor playing the part of the returning prodigal son. I retraced my steps and returned to the service station.

Henry C Weinberg had been out of town at the time of our previous visit. I had very much wanted to meet him and see if he would be able to share some recollections about my father.

After breakfast at our hotel I called his home number. This time he was at home, and I arranged to meet him outside the synagogue on 17th Street at 11.30 am. Before meeting Henry, we decided to explore the excellent railroad museum, which was situated in one of the original railroad workshops buildings in the downtown area. As 11.15 came around we left the museum and headed for our rendezvous on 17th St. We arrived just before the appointed time and, right on cue, Henry drew up in his car. I crossed the street to greet him.

"Good morning Henry, it's a pleasure to meet you at last," I said. Handshakes were followed by a question: "So, what brings you here to Altoona, Norman?"

This query was slightly unexpected, but I was able to answer immediately. "I've come here to learn all I can about my heritage in Altoona and hope you can help me in this quest."

Henry seemed suitably impressed, and he invited us to come into the synagogue, where he would give me an insight into the history and procedures of this place of worship. Although I did not learn anything new about my father in the hour that followed, it was still a worthwhile exercise. Just to be present in the same building where he had attended worship along with his parents and siblings was, in itself, symbolic.

Henry's detailed descriptions and demonstrations of all aspects of Jewish worship were enthralling, and it was plain to see that he was a cornerstone of the present-day Jewish community.

With the synagogue introduction and tour complete, we invited Henry to have lunch with us at a local restaurant. During lunch Charol prompted him for any further recollections about my father. His replies were more or less a repeat of what he had told me the previous year. They were minimal, but the statement that he had "a beautiful voice" had given me a clue to his aspirations and achievements as a radio announcer and disc jockey.

The next port of call was the "Horseshoe Curve" - this time it was open for business and photo opportunities. A short tour of Cresson and Gallitzin followed, and then it was time to head back to Millersville.

The second visit to Altoona had provided a further insight into my father's background. There were, of course, many gaps, and realistically without the person themselves being present, some things will always remain a mystery.

Some days later Charol and Bruce took me on a day trip to New York City. We took the early morning train out of Lancaster, aiming to be in the "Big Apple" around 11 o'clock. Changing trains at Philadelphia and Trenton, we rolled into the city on time. It would take another book to describe the sights we saw that day.

One place in particular had heightened interest for me. My search for my father had uncovered details of his parents' entry into the United States. They had arrived there in 1904 and 1912 respectively and the first place of arrival had been New York City. Now, in 2012, we were going to visit the exact location of their arrival, and on our way we would pass the Statue of Liberty, which would have looked exactly the same all those years ago.

From Battery Park in lower Manhattan we took the ferry to the Statue of Liberty Island. After staying for a while we then re-embarked for the short trip to the former immigration centre, Ellis Island. On the Ellis Island website I had already located my grandparents' names and the microfilm showing their first registration as immigrants entering the US for the first time. To see these buildings in the flesh and to enter the vast hall where everyone had had to wait in line was fascinating.

The hall was known as the registry room. I spotted an information board giving further details - it read: "Nearly every day, for over two decades (1900-24) the Registry Room was filled with new arrivals waiting to be inspected and registered by the Immigration Services. On many days, over 5,000 people would file through this space."

I wondered what these people - including my grandparents - must have thought about whilst waiting. There must have been some apprehension but also excitement, particularly for those of an adventurous character.

All too soon our NYC adventure came to an end, and after a return train journey, we arrived back in Lancaster shortly before midnight. A few days later I flew home from Philadelphia airport at the end of an interesting and educational trip. Before my departure we were all invited to call in at Aunt Marian's apartment, where once more "high tea" was the order of the day. She had uncovered some more photographs of my grandparents, which made for an interesting finale to my trip.

Increasingly now, I had the feeling that my quest was reaching its natural conclusion. Pamela Winfield's words kept coming back to me: "When you embark on a search to discover your biological father, *you must do so with no regrets*". I had none.

Most events in life tend to happen for a reason and my story is a prime example of this theory. There is never a time when you cease to learn lessons through new incidents and experiences.

My recently-discovered American relations are such nice people, and they are a valued part of what was the missing half of my identity. Our cultural and life experiences may have been very different, but the link of family is permanent. Aunt Marian in particular continues to inspire me with her boundless optimism and energy.

This is also a final opportunity to illustrate the wonderful, compassionate human being my mother was. To do this I will use a quotation from Mrs Ivy Jones of New Romney, Kent. When I wrote to Ivy after my mother's passing, the opening line of her reply to me read: "Yes – I was your mother's friend, I can say the family loved her – especially the children, who used to call her Aunty Doris. She was such a good person".

Now the moment is fast approaching for me to let my father's memory also pass into the mists of time. Charol Thompson, when referring to my father following my second visit to Altoona, made this poignant observation: "His footprint seems to have faded away". This is indeed true, and though it is painful to do so, I have to acknowledge this fact.

I feel a deep appreciation of the bravery shown by my father and all his colleagues in having to combat one of the greatest tyrannies ever known to mankind. They left the security of their homeland, travelled thousands of miles and arrived here in the UK ready to assist in the eradication of this evil. Some were destined never to return, and many now lie in a corner of some foreign field, or in the depths of the ocean. For the freedom and prosperity we enjoy today, theirs was the ultimate sacrifice. In the aftermath of this great military operation, many thousands of children – including me – grew up without fathers to love, and from whom to draw inspiration.

At the end of one of his last letters to my mother, my father added the postscript quoted in an earlier chapter: "PS – I may not be at this institution for much longer as I've been given a better offer at another one. If I've left by the time your next letter arrives they'll forward it to me. What price – SUCCESS."

My own letter of farewell to him would read thus:

If success means having to leave behind two people whose admiration, love and loyalty would have endured through both good and bad times, for better or for worse, then the price of success is simply TOO HIGH!

For me your success does not lie where you hoped it would. It lies instead in your wartime exploits. Nothing, but nothing, can diminish their value. Of them I am truly proud. I am proud, too, that your family have accepted me as one of them. That undoubted gain means more to me than any financial success ever could. I should like to think that it makes my mother proud and happy too.

Rest in peace,
Alav ha - shalom
Your loving son,
Norman